Wicked
JOPLIN

LARRY WOOD

Wicked JOPLIN

Charleston  London

THE
History
PRESS

Published by The History Press
Charleston, SC 29403
www.historypress.net

Cover image: Main Street Joplin 1909, color postcard. *Courtesy of Galen Augustus.*

First published 2011

Manufactured in the United States

ISBN 978.1.60949.093.5

Library of Congress Cataloging-in-Publication Data

Wood, Larry (Larry E.)
Wicked Joplin / Larry Wood.
p. cm.
Includes bibliographical references.
ISBN 978-1-60949-093-5
1. Joplin (Mo.)--History. 2. Joplin (Mo.)--Biography. 3. Joplin (Mo.)--Social conditions. 4.
Corruption--Missouri--Joplin--History. 5. Crime--Missouri--Joplin--History. I. Title.
F474.J8W66 2011
977.8'72--dc22
2010051640

CONTENTS

Acknowledgements   7
Introduction   9

Early Growth and the "Reign of Terror"   11
Sinful Sirens—Dutch Em and the Two Mollies   19
Lizzie Bobbitt and the "Enticing" of Kissie West   33
Straight Whiskey with an Edge Like a Buzz Saw   39
Twisting the Tiger's Tail   49
Raising Hell Generally   55
The Boss Beer Man and Other Founding Fathers   61
From Jayhawker to Joplinite   67
A.J. and Cora Johnson and the Vaudeville Variety Theatre   77
Joe Thornton: A Desperado of the Worst Character   87
The Infamous House of Lords   93
One of Those Hot Spots You Get Into and Can't Get Out Of:
    Bonnie and Clyde's Joplin Shootout   99

Epilogue: Joplin's Reputation Through the Years   105
Bibliography   109
About the Author   111

ACKNOWLEDGEMENTS

There are a number of people and organizations who helped make this book a reality that I'd like to thank, and I'll start with the Joplin Public Library, where I did much of my research for the book. I found the entire staff helpful and accommodating, but I want to say thanks to several people in particular. These include Patty Crane, Jason Sullivan, and Jill Halbach-Boswell of the reference section and Leslie Simpson of the Post Memorial Art Reference Library.

The facility where I did most of the rest of my research was the Jasper County Records Center in Carthage, and I owe a special thanks to Steve Weldon and his volunteer staff for making the court records and other documents readily available to me. Steve not only made the records available, but he also provided a couple of photos that I used as illustrations in the book. In addition, he served as the first reader of the manuscript and offered invaluable suggestions. Volunteers at the Records Center who were particularly helpful include Doris Wardlow and Marjorie Bull.

I also want to say a special thank you to Galen Augustus, who provided two images from his postcard collection for use in the book, including the cover image. In addition, I want to thank Brad Belk and the Joplin Museum Complex for supplying a photo of the House of Lords saloon.

I need to mention Jim Hounschell, who gave me directions to the Daniel Sheehan monument at Fairview Cemetery and who otherwise offered me assistance with the chapter on Joe Thornton.

ACKNOWLEDGEMENTS

I also want to thank Jaime Muehl for her thorough and professional edit of the manuscript.

Lastly, I thank my wife, Gigi, who served as a proofreader of the manuscript, as she has for many of my previous works. I thank her, though, not just for her critical eye. Mostly, I thank her for her unwavering support.

INTRODUCTION

When I was growing up in the Springfield area during the 1950s and 1960s, I would occasionally hear an older person comment on Joplin's reputation in former years as a wild, wide-open town. Although I was fascinated by the stories of Joplin's shady past, even as a gullible youth I took them with a dose of skepticism, and by the time I first stepped foot in Joplin about 1964, the town struck me as nearly as tame as any other town. After I moved to Joplin in the mid-1970s, I heard more tales of the town's raucous past, but I still wasn't sure its rowdy reputation was fully warranted. Not until I became interested in regional and local history about twenty years ago and started reading some of the stories from Joplin's early years did I begin to believe, and if I wasn't fully convinced before I started writing this book, I surely am now. What my research revealed is that not only was Joplin known as a wide-open town almost from its birth, and not only did that reputation persist well into the twentieth century, but it was also a reputation that was richly deserved. I trust that some of the stories contained in this book will convince the reader as well.

EARLY GROWTH AND THE "REIGN OF TERROR"

There were naturally many rough characters, who, having everything their own way, created many disturbances, and gave the place an unenviable reputation.
—*F.A. North's 1883* History of Jasper County, *speaking of the early days of Joplin prior to incorporation*

Lead was discovered in southwest Missouri before the Civil War, and mining camps like French Point and Granby sprang up. The war slowed extraction of the mineral in the region, but prospecting resumed in earnest after the fighting ended. Joplin had its beginnings in the late summer of 1870 when miners E.R. Moffett and John B. Sergeant struck ore and built a smelter in the Joplin Creek Valley of southwestern Jasper County on land they had leased the previous spring from John C. Cox, an early settler in the area. Cox had named the creek years before after a friend and fellow settler, the Reverend Harris Joplin, and the mining camp that arose after Moffett and Sergeant struck ore about six hundred feet north of the present-day Broadway viaduct took the name of the creek.

By the beginning of 1871, approximately twenty miners were prospecting in the Joplin Creek Valley, and the growth of the fledgling camp accelerated during the following spring and summer. Around the first of July, John C. Cox laid out a town east of the Moffett and Sergeant diggings that, as the editor of the *Carthage Banner* noted wryly, "he dignified with the name of Joplin City." Meanwhile, Patrick Murphy, arriving from Carthage, organized a town

City of Joplin historic marker near Joplin Creek, where Moffett and Sergeant struck lead in 1870.

company and laid out Murphysburg on the west side of the creek. Cox's plat was filed for record on July 28, 1871, and Murphy's on September 4, 1871.

After first noting the presence of the new mining camp in late June, the *Banner* editor paid the two "towns" a visit in early August expecting to see perhaps a dozen men working the mines, and he was surprised to find instead approximately five hundred. Most of the miners were living in tents or hastily constructed box houses, as Joplin and Murphysburg contained only two permanent houses apiece. Some of the men were making up to forty or fifty dollars a day (an unheard-of amount in 1871), and they were taking lead out of the ground faster than it could be smelted.

The rapid growth continued throughout 1871, and by the end of the year, the two towns boasted a population of almost two thousand people. The total was about equally divided between Joplin City and Murphysburg, and an intense rivalry grew up between them.

Neither Joplin nor Murphysburg had any local government or law enforcement, and with the miners left to police themselves, virtually anything went. The winter of 1871–72 came to be known as the "Reign of Terror." According to Joel Livingston's *History of Jasper County*, the miners about the camp lived "in a constant state of excitement, and without the

JOPLIN CAPITOL!

Removed! Removed! Removed!

S. B. CORN,

HAS REMOVED HIS HEAD-QUARTERS

TO JOPLIN,

——Where he intends to offer one of the——

Largest Stocks of Goods ever offered in this Mining Dist.

Miners and Farmers, look to your Interests, and buy your Goods of

251   S. B. CORN, Joplin, Mo.

A merchant announces to readers of a Carthage newspaper his move to Joplin during the 1871 stampede to the booming mining camp.

refining influence of the home...plunged into a continuous round of merry-making and the lawless element, unrestrained by the officers, had everything their own way. Men who lived on the excitement of frontier life flocked to the new town."

According to Livingston, rough-and-tumble characters with colorful names like "Three Fingered Pete," "Reckless Bill," and "Rocky Mountain Bob" frequented the camps "attired in regular western frontier style. Street fights were common occurrences, and occasionally the excitement was heightened by a shooting scrap." Considering the lawless conditions, however, there were very few murders, and most of the rowdiness was "good-natured revelry."

Initially, the large majority of the people who flocked to Joplin and Murphysburg were single men or married men unaccompanied by their families who hoped to strike it rich in the mines, but businessmen, gamblers, prostitutes, and assorted adventurers soon followed. By the end of 1871, as the place began to take on a semblance of permanency, some of the miners had started bringing their families, and citizens began to see the need for a local government and officers to enforce the law.

Near the end of January 1872, a desperado calling himself "Dutch Pete" had been terrorizing Murphysburg when a strong, athletic miner named J.W. "Bill" Lupton took it upon himself to corral the rebel rouser. Although warned not to mess with "Dutch Pete," Lupton sauntered boldly up to the culprit and, after a furious struggle, threw him to the floor, disarmed him, and tied him up. The incident spurred the citizens to action and helped put an end to the "Reign of Terror." A public meeting was held, and the people passed a resolution petitioning the county court for organization of a township in southwest Jasper County. At the February session of the court, Galena Township, encompassing all of present-day Joplin and stretching to the Kansas state line, was established, and J.W. Lupton, upon the recommendation of the people, was appointed constable. (The size of Galena Township was later reduced when Joplin Township, which includes the eastern portion of present-day Joplin, was established.)

Also in February, the citizens of Joplin and Murphysburg decided it would be in their best interest to join together as one town. The following month the two communities were incorporated under the name Union City, and J.W. Lupton was made marshal. The merger did not do away with the rivalry and ill will between the two towns, however. Feeling aggrieved at what they perceived as unequal treatment by Union City officials, some citizens of the former Joplin City petitioned the county court to have the incorporation dissolved. The request was granted in December 1872, and the old names of Joplin and Murphysburg were restored. The majority of citizens, however, still favored joining together as one town. In a peacemaking gesture, Patrick Murphy, founder of Murphysburg, suggested the name Joplin, and early in 1873 the two towns were incorporated as Joplin.

The incorporation of Union City and later Joplin brought a semblance of order to the area, but as reckless and daring characters kept flocking to the booming mining town throughout the mid-1870s, Joplin continued to witness more than its share of lawless deeds and rowdy behavior.

Usually the fights that characterized early-day Joplin erupted spontaneously and involved mineral rights, a woman, alcohol, or a combination thereof, but occasionally fisticuffs were staged for the mere entertainment of spectators. An issue of the *Union City Mining News* in August 1872 described what the reporter disparagingly referred to as "a disgraceful affair called a prize fight" that had been held the previous Sunday afternoon about a mile outside town. "But one round was fought, and neither of the belligerents was badly hurt."

A particularly notorious incident from Joplin's early days occurred during the time the town was transitioning from Union City. On Sunday, February 16, 1873, a couple of roughs named Edward Atkins and Michael Davis, who had been drinking and carousing together since the night before, paid a visit to Elizabeth Greenma's bar and "boardinghouse" in the tenderloin district of East Joplin about ten o'clock in the morning, and Atkins got into an argument with a man named Edward Daugherty, who had been making his home at

Lizzie's place for some months. According to Davis's later testimony, the quarrel started because Daugherty and Lizzie Greenma were arguing, and Atkins interceded on Lizzie's behalf, but Lizzie herself painted Atkins, whom she characterized as "a gentleman" when he was sober but "awful rough" when he was drunk, as the aggressor. Daugherty told Atkins several times to leave him alone, but Atkins kept pestering Daugherty over a period of several hours and, at one point, even threatened to kill him. Finally, about two or three o'clock in the afternoon, the two exchanged angry words, and Daugherty pulled a pistol out of his pocket and shot Atkins in the stomach when Atkins grabbed hold of him. Atkins managed to knock Daugherty down even after he had been shot and fell on top of him. Daugherty got loose and began beating Atkins until Atkins staggered to his feet, announced that he was "shot through the paunch," collapsed, and died shortly afterward.

Later in the year, Daugherty was found guilty of second-degree murder in the case and sentenced to fifteen years in prison. Lizzie Greenma was indicted as an accessory after the fact to the crime for harboring Daugherty and was briefly jailed, but the case against her was nol-prossed.

Another infamous event in Joplin's early history involved Marshal Lupton, the town's chief law enforcement officer. During early May 1874, Lupton was charged with embezzlement and malfeasance in office, the specification being that he had collected fines from a number of gamblers and women of ill repute and had not accounted for the money but rather pocketed it himself. Lupton denied the charge, but the city council voted to remove him from office and appointed W.B. McCracken to take his place. Lupton, who had been appointed by the county court, claimed the city council did not have the power to try the case and refused to vacate the office.

Upon being assigned his new duty on May 6, McCracken went to the city jail, located in the "Bottoms" along Broadway between East Joplin and West Joplin. (Unlike today, Broadway referred only to the connecting link that crossed Joplin Creek and joined the two Main Streets on the opposite sides of town, and there was no viaduct, only a small bridge, over Joplin Creek. The valley on either side of the creek came to be known as the Kansas City Bottoms, or simply the "Bottoms," after a group of businessmen from the Kansas City area, including John H. Taylor, came to Joplin during the town's very early days and invested heavily in mining along the stream.) According to Dolph Shaner's *The Story of Joplin*, the jail's location on Broadway proved convenient not only because it was easily accessible for both East Joplin and West Joplin but also because the many questionable resorts situated along the street gave rise to a disproportionate number of disturbances. "Broadway...was really a tough spot...Along the south side of its half mile were located saloons, gambling houses, dance halls, Johnson's variety show, and 'honkytonks' such as the Mansion, Dutch Lem's [*sic*], Big Moll's, Little Maude's, and the Red Onion."

When McCracken arrived at the jail, he found it locked and began trying to pick the lock. Lupton happened upon the scene and asked McCracken what he was doing. McCracken informed him that he had been appointed marshal and that he was trying to get into the jail. Taking out a big brass key, Lupton told McCracken he needn't go to the trouble of picking the lock. Lupton opened the door, shoved McCracken inside, and quickly closed and locked it, making the new marshal his prisoner. After being locked up for a few hours, McCracken offered to resign as marshal if Lupton would let him out of jail. Lupton released the prisoner, and McCracken promptly turned in his resignation to the city council, which then appointed W.S. Norton as the new marshal.

Norton proved more determined than McCracken. Recruiting a couple of deputies, he marched to the jail and took the hinges off the door and removed it. Leaving the two deputies to stand guard at the jail, he took the door to a local blacksmith and had new hinges and hasps made. While Norton was away, Lupton showed up at the jail with two of his friends and overpowered the two deputies Norton had left there. When the new marshal returned and saw what had occurred, he drew his revolver and started toward Lupton, who drew his weapon, too, and advanced to meet the threat. Justice of the peace I.W. Davis quickly stepped between the two combatants, commanding "peace in the name of the state." A bloody showdown was averted and a temporary truce agreed upon.

The city council now began ouster proceedings against Lupton in the Jasper County Court at Carthage. On June 3, the court decided in the council's favor and issued an order for Lupton to vacate the marshal's office, but Lupton immediately appealed the decision to the circuit court. That evening a large group of Lupton's friends assembled at the Joplin city jail with the intention of taking possession of it. "The crowd was in an ugly mood," recalled Joel Livingston years later, "and it looked for a time as if there was going to be a battle between the ex-marshal's friends and the law-and-order posse which was assembled at the city hall."

The riot act was read to the angry mob, and city attorney John W. McAntire gave a speech informing them of the court's decision in favor of the city. They grudgingly dispersed, but the next day when Lupton returned from Carthage, he announced that the issue had not yet been decided because he had appealed it. A mass meeting of his friends was called for five o'clock that afternoon for the purpose of passing resolutions condemning the city council and also retaking the city jail. Long prior to the appointed hour, people gathered and began milling around on the streets, and again "it looked as if trouble could not be averted."

The city attorney informed the people that Lupton's appeal did not matter—that the county court's decision would stand unless and until it was overturned by the higher court. The friends of Lupton insisted that the writ of ouster had not been issued but was being held in abeyance pending the outcome of his appeal. The city attorney asked the crowd if they would desist in their demands and disperse if he brought them a certified copy of the ouster decree. They agreed to do so, and McAntire made a flying trip to Carthage in a wagon and team supplied by a local liveryman and returned with the writ just as the planned meeting was getting started. The people agreed to adjourn, and the ousted marshal agreed to await the outcome of his appeal. Lupton later won the appeal and was reinstated, and the events surrounding his ouster were soon being remembered, almost with amusement, as the "Lupton riot."

Recalling the years between 1874 and 1876, Livingston noted that, although the organization of city government had brought the "Reign of Terror" to an end, "Joplin was still about the liveliest place between the Mississippi River and the Rocky Mountains and, while the city was comparatively free from murders and robberies, about everything else was permitted."

What he failed to say was that, in 1876, Joplin's "liveliest" times were yet to come. Lead mining would continue to boom throughout the late 1870s and early 1880s, the town would continue to prosper, and Joplin's reputation as an "evil" place would reach its zenith.

SINFUL SIRENS—DUTCH EM AND THE TWO MOLLIES

*We venture to assert that there is no city in the United States that allows
lewd women as much latitude to pursue their sinful avocations as does Joplin.*
—Joplin Daily Herald, *May 14, 1880*

In America's frontier days, anywhere young single men congregated in large
numbers—be they soldiers, cowboys, or miners—"fallen women" were
sure to show up. Joplin was no exception. Bawdyhouses and prostitutes were
commonplace almost from the town's very beginnings.

One of the very early madams, Lizzie Greenma, was involved in the 1873
murder case described in the previous chapter. In March of the following year,
she was cited in Jasper County Circuit Court for keeping a bawdyhouse and
selling liquor without a license, and a warrant for her arrest was issued when
she failed to appear. (She had probably skipped town, as no further record of
Lizzie Greenma has been located.)

During the March 1874 term of court at which Lizzie was indicted for
keeping a bawdyhouse, James Campbell and his wife, Mary J. Campbell, were
indicted on six counts of the same offense. Like Lizzie, they failed to appear,
and their fine of one dollar for each offense plus court costs was taken out
of the bond that James Cox, son of John C. Cox, and another man had put
up for them.

Other madams of early-day Joplin included Bertha Brooks, Alice Snyder,
and Martha Bynum, all of whom were indicted for keeping bawdyhouses
during 1874 or 1875. The peak of prostitution, though, like the heyday of

other vices, was yet to come. Dutch Em and the two Mollies, the Cyprian queens of Joplin, had yet to come on the scene. Mollie Fisher, Mollie "Big Moll" Tate, and Emma "Dutch Em" Enslinger made their appearance in Joplin during the mid- to late 1870s and reigned over the bordellos of Broadway until the early 1880s. The three were cited in Jasper County Circuit Court numerous times during this period for keeping bawdyhouses and for selling liquor without licenses.

Mollie Fisher was first indicted in September 1876 for keeping a bawdyhouse, and in March of the following year she was charged for the same offense in two separate cases. One of the indictments also carried a charge of selling liquor without a license. Witnesses called in the latter case included Mollie Thomas, Josie Bauer, Georgia Price, and Annie Thatcher, four of the girls who worked out of the defendant's house. The liquor charge and one of the charges of keeping a bawdyhouse were dismissed, but Mollie Fisher pled guilty and paid a twenty-five-dollar fine on the second bawdyhouse charge. At the September 1877 term of court, Mollie was cited in separate cases for maintaining a house of prostitution and for selling liquor without a license. In December 1877, she was charged yet again with keeping a bawdyhouse, and as usual, she was let off with a light sentence. This time it was a fifteen-dollar fine.

Although technically a crime, prostitution was usually not prosecuted vigorously. City and county officials saw it more as a source of revenue than a virulent nuisance that had to be eliminated, and law officers and the courts adopted a simple fine system for dealing with it. The madams and soiled doves paid the fines and were then allowed to resume their enterprise. The fines were usually assessed at the end of each month, and those unable to pay were hauled en masse into police court. A *Joplin Daily Herald* reporter described one such gathering on the first day of February 1878:

> *The court-room had the appearance of a hospital for hungry females...Some were gay, dashing, and shamefully brazen-faced, while others were sad, gloomy and wore a dejected look. Some were dressed in the height of fashion and strutted before judicial eyes in silks and satins flashily decked with pearl, ivory, and dazzling pinchbeck jewelry, while there were others clad in dilapidated calico unadorned with even a "paste-sparkle."*

Mollie Tate set up business in Joplin about the same time as Mollie Fisher. She was first cited in March 1877 on a charge of keeping a bawdyhouse and

Capias--Warrant from Circuit Court for any Indictment.

(Wagner's Statutes, page 1092, sec. 32.)

STATE OF MISSOURI,

County of *Jasper* } ss.

THE STATE OF MISSOURI, To the Sheriff of *Jasper* _____ County, Greeting:

We command you to take *Mollie Tate*

if he be found in your County, and him safely keep, so that you have his body before the Judge of our Circuit Court, at the Court House in *Carthage*

within and for the said County of *Jasper* _____ on the *Second*

Monday in *March* _____ next, then and there, before our said Judge, to answer an

indictment preferred against him by the Grand Jurors of the State of Missouri, empanneled, sworn and

charged to inquire in and for the body of the County of *Jasper*

aforesaid for *Unlawfully setting up and Keeping Bawdy House*

whereof he stands indicted. And this you shall in no wise omit. And have you then and there this writ.

WITNESS my hand as Clerk, and the seal of our said Court hereto

affixed. Done at office in *Carthage* _____ in

the County aforesaid, on this *28th*

day of *January* _____ A. D. 187 *9*

H. H. Williams _____ CLERK.

A Jasper County arrest warrant for Mollie Tate on a charge of keeping a bawdyhouse.

a separate charge of selling liquor without a license during the same term of court at which Mollie Fisher was cited for like offenses. Coincidentally, the witnesses called in the case against Mollie Tate were the same four girls summoned to testify in Mollie Fisher's case, suggesting that the two madams may have been partners operating out of the same house at this time. In September 1877, Mollie Tate was cited for selling liquor without a license, and later in the year she was charged twice more with keeping a bawdyhouse.

Apparently Mollie did a pretty lively business because a notice that she took out in the *Daily Herald* in early March 1878 suggests that she was fairly well off financially. After informing readers that on February 22 she had lost a heavy gold ring with the initials "M.T." engraved on the inside in the vicinity of the Joplin Post Office (at Second and Main), she assured them that the finder of the ring would be "suitably rewarded upon its return to the owner."

Later in March 1878, Mollie was again indicted for keeping a bawdyhouse. One of the witnesses against her, Joseph Logsdon, swore in a deposition, "I know Mollie Tate. I think she controls and runs a house of prostitution. She has the general reputation of landlady of a house of prostitution. I have seen men go to her house. I think they go to visit prostitutes."

In December 1878, Mollie was again indicted for keeping a bawdyhouse, the principal witness against her being Joplin city marshal Cass Hamilton. A year later, in December 1879, she pled guilty to another charge of maintaining a house of ill fame and paid an obligatory twenty-dollar fine.

Mollie Tate died about the first of May 1880, and a new charge of keeping a bawdyhouse that was pending against her at that time was dropped. (The exact date and cause of her death are not known, but her body was shipped back to Cincinnati, where she was buried on May 7 at the Spring Grove Cemetery.) The size of Mollie's estate, which went through probate court shortly after her death, suggests, like the newspaper notice about the lost ring, that she was far from destitute. Perhaps more interesting than the assets she left, though, are the debts she owed. She evidently had been extended credit by a number of Joplin businesses, which now, after her death, sought payment from her estate. Found among the papers in her probate file, for example, was a bill from G. Schmierer, wholesale dealer in liquors, wines, and cigars, for three hundred cigars, three gallons of bourbon, and one case of beer, with which she presumably plied her customers.

On an evening in mid-March 1878, Marshal Hamilton told a Joplin newspaperman that he was going to "raid the brothels" and invited the reporter to go along on the tour of "Joplin by gaslight." The reporter's account of his experience, which appeared in the March 16 *Daily Herald* under the heading

"Sinful Sirens," suggests the prevalence of prostitution in Joplin at the time the two Mollies ran their brothels and also sheds further light on the fine system by which law officers attempted to control it.

"Many of the inmates are behind with fines," Hamilton told the reporter as the pair started out together on a dark, rainy night, "and complaints are being made. This is the last day, and it is absolutely necessary that something must be done, or you wouldn't catch me taking such a tramp such a night as this." The reporter added by way of explanation to his readers that the "courtezans" were required to pay a certain amount of money each month as a fine and that "failure to do so insures [*sic*] their incarceration in the city prison." The fine system, in effect, amounted to a de facto licensing system.

In describing his and the marshal's visits to the first three brothels, the reporter sought to impress upon his readers the filthy conditions of the houses and the shame and misery of the occupants. He claimed that some of the houses were so dirty that "the 'raiders' preferred to stand in the rain and give notices" rather than entering the buildings. After describing the first three visits in some detail, the newspaperman summarized the remainder of the tour:

> *Plunging again into the mud, rain and darkness, the officer and reporter continued their rounds, the former collecting fines at some places, and at others leaving orders for them to appear at court next morning, which meant, come prepared to pay or to go to the cooler. On every hand misery was plainly visible, and while some drowned their misery in tears, others drowned theirs in profanity and vulgarity.*

The pair completed their rounds in an hour, the officer having "done his duty as the law required" and the reporter having "gathered the material for an item."

Prostitution was tolerated with a wink and a nod in early-day Joplin as long as the working girls were discreet, but if they grew too bold or clashed with "respectable" citizens, especially if the "women of easy virtue" happened to be black (as only a few of them were), they risked incurring the wrath of city officials and persons of influence. For instance, a newspaperman, presumably the same reporter who had accompanied Marshal Hamilton on his rounds of the bawdyhouses in March 1878, complained in the *Daily Herald* during late May of the same year, "A colored prostitute, in the company of a supposed respectable white woman, made Main Street lively last night with her vulgarity." The newspaperman also reported in the same issue that "two soiled, sable streetwalkers grossly insulted a lady on Third Street last night" and that the night watchman had to intervene to restore order. (Whether the prostitute who made Main Street lively was also one of the streetwalkers on Third Street is not known.)

Emma Enslinger (sometimes shortened to Ensling) apparently came to Joplin a year or two after the two Mollies. She was indicted for the first time in Jasper County for keeping a bawdyhouse in June 1879 and was charged with the same offense in December of the same year. She paid a twenty-dollar fine and went back to her sporting ways.

On the evening of May 12, 1880, two of Emma's girls, Nettie Perkins and Josie Richmond, were involved in an incident on the streets of West Joplin that again drew the ire of a *Daily Herald* reporter. While walking down Main Street, the two "faded beauties" noticed an elderly gentleman a few yards ahead of them. As soon as they drew beside the man, "one of these ancient damsels of the alleys pushed her companion against him with such force as to knock him off his feet. Laughing with that peculiar brazen horse laugh at his discomfiture, they passed on, jeering as they went."

In June 1880, Emma Enslinger, often called Dutch Em because of her German nativity, was again charged with keeping a bawdyhouse. She pled guilty and paid a twenty-dollar fine. This was near the time that the 1880 census was enumerated. At that time, the twenty-eight-year-old Emma was living on Broadway, and her occupation was given on the census as "Keeps house Prostitution." Living in her household were nineteen-year-old Nettie Perkins, twenty-three-year-old Josie Richmond, twenty-four-year-old Gertrude Hearst, and twenty-three-year-old Mollie Thomas, each of whose occupation was listed as "prostitute."

In October 1880, a man named H.W. Shannon, presumably a gentlemen caller at the Broadway brothel, filed a complaint against Emma Enslinger, charging her with grand larceny. Bud Fagg, a notorious gambler and general ne'er-do-well, and Allie Rogers, who was very likely one of Emma's girls, were also implicated in the crime. The specification was that the defendants had taken two diamond studs, two $100 bank notes, one $100 treasury note, one $50 silver certificate, and ten $20 bills from the plaintiff. Allie and Dutch Em were arrested, but Bud Fagg, not surprisingly, was nowhere to be found. However, among the witnesses for the defense who did appear at the preliminary hearing in December was Nettie Perkins. The court was apparently unimpressed by the plaintiff's case, or maybe the court's reasoning was simply that he got what he deserved for cavorting with whores. At any rate, after the evidence was presented, the complaint was dismissed, the defendants discharged, and Shannon ordered to pay court costs.

At the same term of court at which the charge of larceny against her was heard, Dutch Em pled guilty to keeping a bawdyhouse and paid a fifteen-dollar fine. She was charged again with the same offense in mid-1882, the indictment specifying that she had kept a bawdyhouse in Joplin on or about the fifteenth of June and at "divers other times." Emma was last accused of keeping a bawdyhouse in Joplin in June 1883.

Not long after the latter date, Em's place was destroyed by fire. Shaner's *The Story of Joplin* recounts a farcical yarn that was told to the author years after the fact about Em running out of her burning building in a Mother Hubbard (a loose, shapeless dress) carrying a pillow and a slop jar. The firemen, when they saw her, could not resist turning the hose on her. Cursing them angrily, Em yelled, "Turn the water on the house, you fools! I'm not on fire."

Emma Enslinger apparently took her leave of the bagnios of Joplin shortly after her house burned, since her name does not appear in Jasper County records after 1883.

Another Joplin madam during the era of Dutch Em and the two Mollies was Lillie Wiggans, who was charged in August 1878 with keeping a house of prostitution. In June 1880, she was indicted again for keeping a bawdyhouse and paid a twenty-dollar fine. At the time of the 1880 census, Lillie was living on Virginia Avenue and was enumerated as head of a household that also included nineteen-year-old Frankie Martin, nineteen-year-old Ida May, and eighteen-year-old Ada Jones. The occupation of all four women was given as "prostitute" on the census. Also living in the household were a twenty-seven-year-old woman and a fourteen-year-old girl, each of whose occupation was listed as "servant." In December 1880, Lillie was again indicted for keeping a bawdyhouse. She pled guilty and paid a fifteen-dollar fine. She was charged again with the same offense a year later, in December 1881.

Sometimes a young woman who started out as a working girl graduated to the status of madam. Such was the case with Mollie Thomas, who was listed as a prostitute in the household of Emma Englinger at the time of the 1880 census and earlier had been called as a witness in cases involving both Mollie Fisher and Mollie Tate. (The fact that Mollie Thomas and some of the other girls were associated at various times with different madams suggests that prostitution in early-day Joplin was a close-knit sorority in which the girls and the madams probably all knew one another.) Mollie Thomas was charged with keeping a bawdyhouse in May 1883, over six years after she had first been mentioned in connection with prostitution in Joplin. Considering that most of the ladies of the night came and went with regularity, Mollie's tenure as a scarlet woman of Joplin likely lasted longer than that of almost any other.

Nearly all of the prostitutes of early Joplin were young women in their late teens and early twenties. An exception was forty-year-old Sarah Hill, who was listed on the 1880 census as a prostitute and was living alone in a house on Virginia at the time.

Gauged by the ratio of prostitutes to total population, the late 1870s and early 1880s may rightly be considered the heyday of whoredom in Joplin, but in terms of sheer numbers the apogee may have come later. Joplin kept growing rapidly over the next twenty or thirty years, and ladies of the evening continued to ply their trade almost unabated well into the next century, even as the town increasingly took on the trappings of respectability like churches, schools, and community organizations. Lead and zinc mining in the region did not peak until after the turn of the twentieth century, and as long as hotblooded young miners continued to populate the town, there were bound to be plenty of joy girls to service them.

During Joplin's very early years, the houses of ill repute were concentrated along Main Street of East Joplin and along Broadway. (Lillie Wiggans's place on Virginia Avenue was near that street's intersection with Broadway.) Apparently there was some attempt by the town's "respectable" citizens to confine prostitution to these areas. The *Daily Herald* of September 20, 1879, reported, "A house on Pearl Street, occupied by a firm of females who traffic in affection, was bombarded last night by stones." The reporter conjectured that the onslaught was made by individuals who "object to having such a despicable avocation carried on in that vicinity."

By the late 1880s, however, West Joplin had already outpaced the east side to become the town's primary business district, and the tenderloin district inevitably shifted slightly west as well. While the red lights still shone on Broadway, Main Street in West Joplin arose as a secondary site for prostitution. A local legend that another of Joplin's main thoroughfares, Maiden Lane, located about a mile west of Main Street, was so named because it served during the town's early years as the principal red light district appears to have little basis in fact, because downtown Joplin was always where the action was.

For example, shortly after midnight during the wee hours of July 25, 1887, Joplin police raided the rooms over Perkins's saloon and restaurant located in the 400 block of South Main. According to the *Daily Herald*, the rooms had "become notorious as an assignation house," and the raid yielded "quite a haul of naughty women." Two of the women escaped, but four were captured and hauled to the calaboose to spend the night. Arraigned the next morning at police court on charges of being inmates of a bawdyhouse, they gave their names as Sally Lane, Minne Baker, Stella Anderson, and Kissie Pannel. Sally Lane and Kissie Pannel pled guilty and paid fines and court costs totaling $9.15 each, while the other two women demanded a trial, which was scheduled for the following day. "There will be some racy developments," opined the *Herald* newspaperman, "and police court will have a crowded attendance."

Joplin city officials struggled from the town's very beginning with the issue of how to control prostitution without retarding the growth of the rip-roaring mining town. As early as 1879, the town adopted an ordinance specifying that "any houses kept for the purpose of prostitution or promiscuous sexual intercourse, bawdy and disorderly houses, are declared nuisances." Violators were subject to fines from $5 to $100.

Near the end of 1889, the question of how to handle prostitution arose again. A number of businessmen were concerned that the bawdyhouses on Main Street and Broadway might be a deterrent to their business interests. The businessmen wanted the brothels moved away from the downtown district to a more discreet location, and they suggested regulating the bawdyhouses through a licensing system. In early January 1890, they presented to the city council a petition signed by about two hundred citizens urging such a course of action. The idea, however, met resistance in the city council, where it was pointed out that the businessmen were asking the council to do something it had no legal right to do, since Missouri state statutes explicitly forbade cities from licensing prostitution. A councilman named Norris wanted to crack down on prostitution and try to do away with it altogether. He said the council could not adopt any method of dealing with prostitution that would appear "to sanction an evil and encourage lewdness and crime." The consensus, however, seemed to be to "get back to the old order of things" (i.e. a fine system), and the council meeting ended with no action being taken on the bawdyhouse issue.

Despite occasional public outcries against prostitution, like that of Councilman Norris in 1890, brothels continued to flourish in Joplin. As was the case from the very early days of the town's history, the men who frequented the bordellos tended to be rough characters, so the brothels were often the scene of fistfights or gunplay. In early September 1891, a shooting affray occurred at "a bagnio on Broadway" run by Mollie Collins. (Apparently, about half of all Joplin madams were named Mollie.) The *Joplin Sunday Herald* said the place was "formerly known by the highly picturesque name of the Dirty Dozen. The inmates no doubt are just as filthy now as they were formerly and the only reason perhaps why the old name is not applicable is that now the inmates number less than a dozen."

The confrontation at the erstwhile Dirty Dozen occurred when two rough characters named Mack Applegate and Charlie Stewart called at the house between nine and ten o'clock on the night of September 5 and made themselves too much at home for Mollie's liking. The madam got into a heated argument with Applegate, and he slapped her in the mouth. Mollie promptly called for help, and Applegate took off running as her bouncer, Stanley Clark, appeared on the scene. Shots rang out as Applegate raced out the door and down the street, and a bullet tore into his right shoulder. Hearing the shots, a law officer hurried to the scene, and Applegate, not seriously injured, told the policeman what had happened. Mollie claimed she had fired the shot that wounded Applegate, but Applegate said Clark did it. Both Mollie and her bouncer were arrested and taken to the lockup.

Mr. Norris may have been joined on the council in the early 1890s by other men who did not want the city to sanction prostitution or at least did not want to give such an appearance, because in 1893 the city passed an ordinance strengthening the language of the 1879 statute and increasing the fine for violating it. The new ordinance read in part:

> *Any female person of the age of twelve years or over who shall lodge in or resort to any bawdy house, assignation house or house of ill-fame, for the purpose of prostitution or who for the purpose of plying her vocation as a prostitute, shall stand or wait on any street, alley, sidewalk, lane or other public place within the city...shall be deemed guilty of a misdemeanor.*

Madams, who were dealt with more harshly than the prostitutes themselves, were subject to a fine between $200 and $1,000 for keeping "in this city any house, tent or booth for the purpose of prostitution or promiscuous sexual intercourse."

Such ordinances, though, had little effect. At least some of Joplin's prostitutes, as was often the case elsewhere, were cocaine or morphine addicts, and even more were addicted to alcohol. They were not easily deterred by the threat of a fine, even if it was a stiff one.

For instance, Flo Banks, a lady of pleasure who had a long police record in Joplin around the turn of the twentieth century, was reportedly a "cocaine fiend." Also, in July 1898, Mamie Gordon, "an inmate of a north end immoral resort," was found dead in her bed after having taken an overdose of morphine (although her ex-boyfriend claimed she was not in the habit of using the drug). It was reported at the time of her death that the thirty-three-year-old Mamie had come from a well-to-do family near Kansas City. She had married young but deserted her husband after he started abusing her and then entered into "a life of shame."

Most of the prostitutes of Joplin, as was no doubt the case elsewhere, were women like Mamie who were on their own, either having been kicked out of their homes or having left to escape an abusive husband or father. Occasionally, though, an innocent young child would get drawn into the seamy world of prostitution by her scarlet mother. For instance, when Pearl "Cornbread" Wilson, a "well-known police character," was arrested and placed in jail in late November 1903 on a charge of street walking, she began to cry because the deputy would not allow her five-year-old daughter in the cell with her. When a matron from the Children's Home arrived to take the girl away, Pearl was allowed momentarily out of her cell to tearfully kiss her child goodbye, and a "most pathetic scene was enacted" as the officers finally had to wrench the mother and daughter apart. Later, after Cornbread had been released, she caused a disturbance at the Children's Home in early December and again near Christmas stubbornly trying to regain custody of her child.

A *Joplin Globe* article from June 1905 entitled "Proof that Joplin Needs a Police Matron" suggests that prostitution was still going strong in the town during the first decade of the twentieth century. Citing police records, the

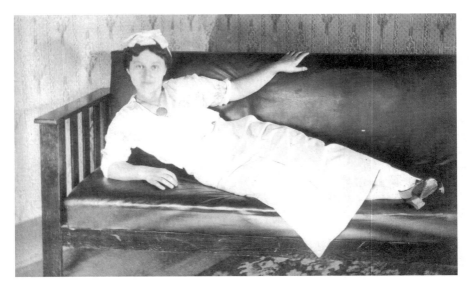

An unidentified prostitute believed to have been involved in a Jasper County divorce case circa 1910. *Courtesy of Jasper County Records Center.*

Globe said eighty women had been arrested in Joplin during the previous month. Of the total, twenty-nine were charged with prostitution, twenty-one with "lewd conduct," and thirteen with street walking. Although it is not known how much the *Globe's* editorializing affected the thinking of the city fathers, Joplin did, in fact, hire a police matron a year later.

In 1908, Jane DeChancy was arrested for keeping "a common bawdy house" at the southeast corner of Second and Main Streets "known as 201 Main Street in the city of Joplin within one hundred yards of a building ordinarily used as a city hall." Her arrest did not deter her from continuing to pursue her vocation, as she was cited several other times between 1908 and 1913 for maintaining a house of ill repute in Joplin, but the effrontery she and others like her showed by locating their houses in the very heart of town, sometimes almost on the doorsteps to the seat of city government, may have helped spur a grand jury investigation into prostitution that the citizens of Joplin undertook in 1911. The jurors found that

> *bawdy houses have been run with the full knowledge and consent of the police department of the City of Joplin, some of said bawdy houses being within a block of the police station. We further find from our investigation of the police judge's docket and from an investigation of city officials that inmates of bawdy houses have been taken to the police station between the hours of one and four A.M. in the morning and assessed a fine of one dollar and costs, total ten dollars; that they have been permitted to return to the bawdy house and continue their whoredom with the full knowledge of the Chief of Police of the City of Joplin; and that they have been arrested a number of times under the present administration and a license given them under the pretense and guise of a fine until objections were raised to such conduct by the Prosecuting Attorney's Office. We further find upon investigation that Virginia Avenue, Second and Third Streets, North Main and Joplin Streets together with A and B Streets, all within a radius of three blocks of the police station, are patrolled by street walkers, street solicitors, pimps and bawds and that appeals have been made to the police department by citizens living in this locality to abate this condition but that no relief has been given the citizens.*

Despite periodic attempts, like the 1911 grand jury investigation, to clamp down on prostitution in Joplin, the scarlet ladies continued to patrol the streets for at least another decade. It was not until Prohibition shut down the saloons and other free-and-easy establishments that prostitution began to diminish in Joplin.

The abatement was hastened by the gradual tapering off of lead and zinc mining in the area during the second quarter of the twentieth century, but the "oldest profession" continued to persist on some level in Joplin for many more years. The evidence is mostly anecdotal, since the city fathers had finally succeeded in driving vice underground to a large degree, but stories abound in the local lore of assignations during World War II, for instance, between soldiers stationed at nearby Camp Crowder and the ladies of the night at wild Joplin. A lifelong resident of Joplin, for example, recently stated that when he was a boy growing up in the town during the war years, a hotel at Third and Virginia Avenue was mockingly called the "Virgin Hotel" because of the many ladies of the night who hung out there and the assignations that took place there.

While researching this book, I was told by at least one individual that places of sexual rendezvous and resort still exist in Joplin if a person is interested enough in finding them. Such an assertion may or may not be true, but one thing is sure—it's not the way it was in the old days when prostitution existed openly with the full knowledge and the tacit approval of city fathers. Those days have long ago been consigned to the annals of Joplin's wild and woolly past.

LIZZIE BOBBITT AND THE "ENTICING" OF KISSIE WEST

*The only place that offered her shelter was the brothel, and her only course
was to give up all hope of happiness in this life, and become a prostitute and
be dishonored and despised by everyone.*
—Joplin Daily Herald, *March 16, 1878*

As the previous chapter demonstrates, Joplin had more than its share
of "sinful sirens" during its early days, but the story of one of them,
Lizzie Bobbitt, stands out as particularly interesting. Elizabeth "Lizzie"
Hall married Henry D. Sanford on May 13, 1871, in Kosciusko County,
Indiana. The couple moved west, but Sanford deserted Lizzie in early 1873.
After her abandonment, Lizzie spent some time in Jefferson City, Missouri,
where, according to a later newspaper report, she "kept a boarding house for
the accommodation of members of the Legislature, from which occupation
she made enough money to purchase some fine furniture." Later, Lizzie lived
in Atchison County, Missouri, where she met J.F. Bobbitt, and he started
trying to win her affections. In late 1874, he told Lizzie that he had studied
the law and that the mere fact that her husband had left her and stayed
away for almost two years constituted a legal divorce. Following Lizzie to
Joplin, he convinced her to enter into what Lizzie later called a "pretended
marriage" with him, and the couple set up housekeeping at the rip-roaring
mining camp of Lone Elm on the north edge of town. Lizzie may have
considered the marriage a sham, but it was solemnized by a minister of the
gospel on December 16, 1874, at the Methodist Episcopal parsonage in

West Joplin and duly recorded in the Jasper County recorder's office early the following year.

Lizzie, though, was apparently unhappy in the relationship from the very beginning, and when she learned in March 1875 that Bobbitt had deceived her in telling her that her first marriage was null and void in the eyes of the law, she announced her intention to leave him. Even though H.D. Sanford had since died, he was alive at the time of her marriage to Bobbitt, and Lizzie, therefore, considered the second marriage fraudulent. Bobbitt responded to her threat to leave by selling some furniture from the Lone Elm home that Lizzie considered hers, and she then carried through on the threat. On May 3, using the name "Lizzie Sanford," she went to the Joplin Court of Common Pleas and filed a replevin suit declaring that she and Bobbitt had been living together in a "pretended marriage" and that certain property at the Lone Elm home and certain other property that Bobbitt had already sold belonged to her. She was granted an "order of delivery," and Jasper County deputy sheriff William Carter executed the order, gathering approximately $80 worth of goods that Lizzie claimed were hers. When it was discovered, however, that J.F. Bobbitt and Lizzie were, in fact, legal husband and wife and that "Lizzie Sanford" was a "fictitious name," Lizzie was charged with forgery and fraud for obtaining goods and chattels under false pretenses. On July 1, she gave bond in the amount of $200 to ensure her court appearance in September, at which time she paid court costs and was let go.

As soon as charges against her were dismissed (or perhaps while she was still awaiting a hearing), Lizzie removed to Newton County and took up residence in a "house of ill-fame" near the train depot in Neosho. On December 23, a seventeen-year-old lad named Lane Britton was lolling away the evening at Lizzie's house when a young man named Huffaker and two drunken companions called at the brothel and asked admittance. Lizzie turned them away, and when they kept trying to gain entrance anyway, Britton shot Huffaker through the door, killing him almost instantly. A warrant on a murder charge was issued for Britton after he fled the scene, and Lizzie Sanford, whom the editor of the *Neosho Times* called an "abandoned strumpet," was arrested as an accessory. The next day she was discharged when the prosecution failed to appear at her scheduled hearing, and the *Times* editor complained in the following week's newspaper that she "now runs at large to flaunt her brazen strumpetry on our streets."

Lizzie lingered in Neosho, though, for no more than a few days. By January 1876, she was back in Jasper County, where she set up residence on Main Street of East Joplin (now Langston Hughes Broadway), and her house, like the one she had kept in Neosho, quickly gained a reputation as a resort for lewd women.

Shortly after Lizzie moved into her home in Joplin, a teenaged girl named Kesiah "Kissie" West came to live with her as a housekeeper or "hired girl." The girl left after only a couple of weeks but soon returned and asked to stay at the house as a prostitute. Lizzie turned her away, absolutely refusing, according to Lizzie's own later testimony, "to maintain her or receive or keep her as an inmate at all." Within a month, however, Kissie came back once again begging to be allowed to stay at the house and work as a prostitute. Lizzie had a long, heart-to-heart talk with the girl, warning her of the shame and ruin that would come to her if she went into a life of prostitution, but Kissie replied that her life was already in a worse condition than that of a prostitute. Kissie said she had been seduced by her stepfather and could not live at home, that she had tried to earn a living on her own but could not make enough money to clothe and feed herself, that she had been having

Warrant for the arrest of Lizzie Bobbitt on a charge of enticing Kissie West into prostitution.

sex with men continually and "getting nothing for it," and that "I had better be here where I can make some money than slinging pots and shagging for nothing as all the girls are who are working at the hotels."

Lizzie relented "out of sympathy for the girl," had her cured of the venereal disease Kissie had contracted during one of her prior cavorts with men, and let the girl join the other sporting women at her establishment. A few days later, Kissie's mother, Permelia West, visited her daughter at Lizzie's house and, according to Lizzie's later testimony, seemed well satisfied with the arrangement.

Mrs. West, though, must have had a change of heart, or perhaps she only later realized the precise nature of what was going on at Lizzie's house, because in September 1876, apparently at the mother's insistence, Lizzie Bobbitt was charged in Jasper County Circuit Court with enticing a girl under the age of eighteen into prostitution. Lizzie gave bond in October and was released to appear in court on the charge the following spring.

At her trial on March 13, 1877, Lizzie was surprised when Permelia West testified that her daughter had not been abandoned but had still been under parental care and guardianship at the time she went to live in the bawdyhouse and that Kissie had moved in with Mrs. Bobbitt against the mother's wishes. Lizzie was also surprised to hear Kissie swear that she had gone to live at the house only because Lizzie had offered her inducements and told her she would be better off. After hearing the testimony of the mother and daughter, the jury found Lizzie guilty and sentenced her to three years in the state penitentiary.

In late March, having gained new information since her trial that she felt would exonerate her and having compiled a list of witnesses willing to testify on her behalf, Lizzie filed a motion for a new trial. Two of her witnesses claimed to have heard Permelia West admit that she had driven her daughter away from home because Kissie "made trouble" between Mrs. West and her husband and that she "would not let the nasty little heifer come home anymore." Another potential witness said similarly that he had heard Mrs. West say she had driven her daughter away because the stepfather was "after her [Kissie] all the time" and that she "thought it better that Kissie had gone into a whorehouse where she could make some money." Several witnesses were also ready to testify that Kissie had not been enticed into prostitution but that she instead had "been living in an open state of lewdness and adultery with certain men in Joplin" long before she came to Lizzie's house and that she came there of her own accord.

In early April, Lizzie's motion for a new trial was initially overruled but was granted upon appeal. Lizzie was released on bond and ordered to appear back in court in October.

Lizzie Bobbitt and the "Enticing" of Kissie West

Free on bond, she apparently went back to her sporting ways as though nothing had happened. In July, she was charged in Jasper County Circuit Court with "keeping a bawdy house or brothel, commonly called a house of ill fame" and "permitting and suffering divers...lewd and dissolute men and women to resort to her house for the purpose of illicit sexual intercourse and there to remain whoring against the peace and dignity of the state of Missouri."

The disposition of the case against Lizzie on the charge of keeping a bawdyhouse is not known, as no record has been found, although she probably paid a fine and was released, as was common. On the more serious charge of "kidnapping" Kissie West, Lizzie was acquitted at her new trial in early October. She apparently left Joplin shortly afterward, since her name does not appear in extant Jasper County Circuit Court records in connection with any additional cases after the July 1877 charge of keeping a brothel. Where she went and what happened to her is unknown, and in 1877 few people probably cared.

STRAIGHT WHISKEY WITH AN EDGE LIKE A BUZZ SAW

Joplin has 11 barber salons and about 117 whiskey shops.
—Springfield Times, *March 20, 1878*

As one might expect of a rough-and-tumble mining camp populated largely by single young men, early-day Joplin was a place where liquor flowed freely. In 1875, the *Joplin News* reported there were seventy-five saloons in town, and other newspapers made similar claims about the same time. While these estimates were exaggerations, one thing is clear: early Joplinites enjoyed their whiskey and beer, and they didn't let minor inconveniences like Sunday closing laws and not having liquor licenses stop them from slaking their thirst.

In fact, the very first business in Murphysburg (i.e. West Joplin) was a saloon. The town's plat had not yet been finalized when Herman Geldmacher showed up in early August 1871 and bought a lot on Main Street between First and Second. According to Livingston's 1912 county history, the business that "Moneymaker," as the miners called him, started was a restaurant and bakery. However, it differed little from Joplin's other saloons, almost all of which served food as well as booze, and Geldmacher's place was referred to as a saloon in 1870s newspapers.

Also, Joplin's first church service was held in a saloon. One day in early 1872, a group of citizens was discussing the need for a church when Kit Bullock, half owner of Bullock and Boucher's saloon on Main Street, jokingly offered the saloon as a sanctuary. Unknown to Bullock, one of the men among the group was an itinerant Methodist minister, who

A Missouri saloon, circa 1900. *Courtesy of Legends of America.*

immediately took the saloonkeeper up on his offer, promising to hold service the next day if Bullock meant what he said. True to his word, Bullock dutifully cleaned up the saloon, replaced the liquor bottles with candles, and stretched plank boards across his beer kegs to form makeshift pews. The next day, the preacher showed up and delivered a sermon to several solemn and presumably sober worshipers.

Moderation in the consumption of alcohol was rare in early Joplin. Liquor was more potent than it is today, and even beer, for those who chose to drink it, was served in large glasses and had a higher alcohol content than nowadays. Explained a *Daily Herald* reporter in 1878:

> *The average Joplin tippler wouldn't care a continental to get drunk unless he got so drunk he couldn't distinguish a street lamp from a new moon or a golden chariot set with diamonds as large as a Carthage girl's foot. It is a custom among Joplin drinkers to take, say "three fingers," ask the bar-keeper for a chew of tobacco and then measure out another drink by the same number of digits. He doesn't want any of your mild beverages, either, such as bitters, beer and lemonade with a center pole, but straight whiskey, and even that must have an edge on it like a buzz-saw, and go down like a torch*

light procession...The drinker has an object in view that cannot be consummated with any other article. He expects to get on the streets and air his lungs; yell like a Texas cow-boy and swear he can whip a ton of wild-cats or any other beasts or prey.

Several of Joplin's earliest saloons, like some of its gambling emporiums and other amusement bazaars, were located in the bottoms on Broadway. Shaner's *The Story of Joplin* offers a vivid picture of them:

The bottoms saloons along the Broadway road connecting the two Main Streets, like old-time fish markets, needed no signs. The odor from stale beer was supplemented by that from Star tobacco boxes used for cuspidors and filled with filthy sawdust...Some bars had brass rails for resting feet encased in buckled shoes; and most had back bar mirrors decorated with female figures by some tramp artist. The usual filthy bull-pen was in the rear.

At least one of the saloons, added Shaner, had a dance hall where "a rough sort of dancing" was engaged in, and in a couple of the tougher dives, "there were some women who danced with men, some women in rouge and large hats with ostrich plumes and shiny black satin skirts," whose main purpose was to increase the consumption of liquor.

Main Street in East Joplin also had several saloons in the very early days, but by the late 1870s, Thomas Connor's Senate Saloon was one of the few drinking establishments that remained in East Town. Another was the 76 Saloon located at the Grandview Hotel.

Not surprisingly, Joplin's saloons were occasionally the stage for fisticuffs or gunplay, like the shooting affray that occurred at the 76 in September 1877. The 76 had a reputation as a "hard place" and a "general rendezvous for the colored boys of East town," but in early September 1877 a new proprietor named Heffler took over the saloon with the intention that "it should no longer be a general resort of the colored men of Joplin." When Thomas Doss and another black man showed up on September 26 to play cards, Heffler tried to put them out or move them to another room. A heated argument ensued, and Heffler ended up shooting Doss through the breast, wounding him seriously but not fatally. Not long afterward, the 76 was moved out of the Grandview and relocated at the east end of Main.

The saloon district, though, had mostly moved to Main Street in West Joplin by the late '70s. Henry Sapp's Miner's Drift, for instance, was located at the northwest corner of Second and Main. The Joplin Hotel saloon (also called the Brick Hotel saloon) at the corner of Fourth and Main was run by William and Hugh Teets, and Thomas Heathwood had a saloon at the corner of Third and Main.

Other early Joplin saloonkeepers included Henry and James Archer, William Bassett, Punch Bell, Henry Blackwell, Frederick Claire, Bernard "Barney" Ferguson, Charley Geltz, William Leffen, Thomas Mayberry, Edward McCallum, John Pabst, Samuel Peeler, Joe Perkins, Gottlieb and John Schmierer, Levi Stauffer, Lafayette "Fate" Vancil, Charles Warrick, Henry and John Willhardt, and Daniel Youngblood.

In some cases, the saloons had simple and fitting names like the Miner's Exchange, while others were known principally by the owner's name. Levi Stauffer's place, for instance, was known only as Levi's Exchange. Most of the saloons, though, had colorful names like the Anchor, the Black Diamond, the Board of Trade, the Cyclone, the Globe, the Golden Gate (also at the corner of Third and Main), the Last Chance, the North Star, the Palace, the Port Royal, the Steamboat, and the Willow Branch. The latter place was owned by Sam Peeler, and John Pabst ran the Port Royal.

In many cases, however, it is difficult to know exactly which saloonkeepers were associated with which saloons, because the saloonkeepers came and went with regularity and the saloons frequently changed names. For instance, John Schmierer, who, along with his brother Gottlieb Schmierer, was an early saloonkeeper and liquor dealer in Joplin, moved to Galena (Kansas) in the summer of 1879 and opened a saloon there before returning to Joplin less than two years later and taking over the saloon previously run by Charley Geltz.

Suffice it to say that early Joplin boasted an abundance of saloons, especially for a town with only a few thousand people, but the number of drinking establishments did not match some of the inflated estimates. When Barney Ferguson rented a storeroom that previously had housed the Lichlyter Brothers Grocery to a Texas man so that he could put in a saloon in the spring of 1879, the *Daily Herald* commented that the new saloon would make over twenty saloons in Joplin and "still there's room for more." A year later, when Fate Vancil and one of the Archers opened a new saloon, the *Herald* counted it as the nineteenth saloon in Joplin. These are no doubt more creditable figures than the *Joplin News*'s 1875 exaggeration. Prior to 1880, the number of saloons in Joplin probably did not exceed twenty-one or twenty-two at any given time, but this was still a high ratio of saloons to people, considering that the total population of Joplin in 1880 was no more than approximately ten thousand, including women, children, and abstemious men.

Joplin officials made at least a token effort to control the town's liquor commerce. An 1870s ordinance, for instance, declared that anyone selling intoxicating liquors in quantities less than a gallon must take out a dram license. The cost of the license was thirty dollars per quarter. However, the incentive to abide by the law was not particularly great, since the usual fine for selling liquor without a license was only forty dollars or so. Most of the law's violators were saloonkeepers who had let their licenses lapse or had failed to take one out in the first place, but other business owners, particularly druggists, were sometimes guilty of selling liquor without a license.

For example, Thomas Donahoo, who ran a drugstore in the Berz Building at the northeast corner of Fourth and Main, was cited about 1878 for selling liquor without a license. Several men who had been served alcohol at the store or who otherwise had pertinent knowledge were deposed in support of the charge. One man said he had seen men go into the back of Dr. Donahoo's store and "come out smacking their lips." Another testified that he himself had been served liquor at Donahoo's on more than one occasion and that a drink generally cost ten cents. He said that a man could get whiskey either by going into the store and asking for it straight out or by saying that he needed some "medicine." The customer would then generally be taken into a back room and served a drink of liquor.

There was also a law against businesses remaining open on Sunday, but it was only periodically enforced. So again, the incentive to abide by it was not great. Saloonkeepers were occasionally cited for staying open or selling liquor on Sunday but not frequently enough to keep them from doing the same thing the next weekend, because the usual fine of five dollars served as little deterrent.

One of the early multiple offenders of Joplin's liquor laws was Punch Bell. As early as April 1872, Punch was cited in Jasper County Circuit Court on five different charges of selling liquor without a license. It's unclear which saloon he was associated with at this time, but later in the '70s he was part owner of Levi's Exchange. In the summer of 1879, he sold his interest in the place to his partner, Levi Stauffer, and announced that he was quitting the saloon business.

Another frequent offender of the early liquor laws was Henry Sapp of the Miner's Drift. He was charged repeatedly throughout the 1870s and early 1880s for selling liquor on Sunday and at least a time or two for selling liquor without a license.

The Miner's Drift, like many of the early saloons, had billiard tables as an added inducement to draw customers. Some of the saloons, on the

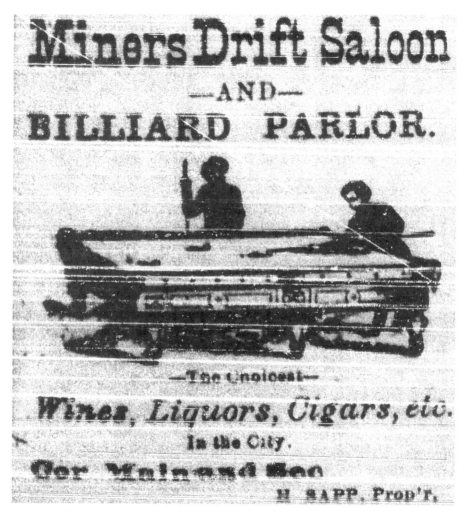

Ad for Henry Sapp's Miner's Drift Saloon that appeared in an 1880 Joplin newspaper.

other hand, went to bizarre lengths to attract crowds. In November 1876, for instance, Blackwell's saloon staged a fight between six full-blooded bulldogs and a Cinnamon bear brought up from the Arkansas hills for the entertainment of patrons. Twelve hundred people reportedly watched the brawl, which the bear won.

However, the main attraction, besides liquor, at nearly all the saloons was food. Most of the Joplin saloons doubled as restaurants, similar to today's bar and grill establishments, and many of them periodically served free meals. Their customers were expected to drink enough liquor to justify the outlay, and there were only a few men in Joplin who were what the *Daily Herald* called "lunch fiends," or men who abused the good will of the saloonkeepers.

During the summer of 1879, Henry Sapp started setting up a free lunch every evening at 10:00 p.m., and it was reported that he received "visits from all the night owls." The nocturnal meals were evidently a hit, because later in the summer Sapp announced that he was going to start staying open all night.

The late nights, though, must have taken their toll. Like Punch Bell, Sapp tired of tending bar after a number of years, and he sold the Miner's Drift to Billy Beller in the spring of 1881. Sapp later returned to the saloon business in Joplin for at least a brief period, and Beller was still operating at Sapp's old location at 124 South Main in 1895.

Despite the *Daily Herald*'s facetious disclaimer to the contrary, early Joplinites enjoyed beer as well as hard liquor. Beer was especially popular among the town's large German population; in fact, several of the saloonkeepers were German. For several years during Joplin's early history, the town observed Bock Beer Day, an ancient custom originating in the southern part of the German Empire in observation of which, explained the *Daily Herald*, "all good and loyal beer drinkers celebrate the first day of May by imbibing large quantities of Bock beer." On the appointed day in 1880, "All the subjects of King Gambrinus [the patron saint of beer] assembled at the saloons" in Joplin and

> *poured down all the Bock beer they could possibly hold...Bock beer is considerably stronger than ordinary beer, and consequently has more of a tendency to produce temporary insanity, and sometimes it causes the mildest mannered citizen to mash up his furniture and play the part of a Comanche Indian on the warpath. Bock beer is a very fine drink, but the price paid is usually a sad case of "bust head."*

A public beer garden was located at Turkey Creek on the northeast outskirts of town, and it proved a particularly popular destination for weekend getaways, especially when city officials chose to enforce the law against saloons staying open on Sunday, as they did in late June 1880. "The saloon men are complaining of another severe attack of city ordinance," a *Daily Herald* reporter said. On the previous Sunday, the newspaperman added, "If the boys wanted anything to take, they had to go to the beer garden for it."

Joplin had a reputation early on as an intemperate place and was sometimes the butt of jokes because of its excess. A Carthage newspaper reported in the summer of 1877, "The supply of beer ran out in Joplin Saturday night and by Monday the inhabitants were well nigh burned up. Steps have been taken to provide against such a calamity in the future."

A temperance crusade called the Murphy Movement that had been sweeping the country for over a year reached the Ozarks in early 1878 and won hundreds of converts in Springfield, Carthage, and other area towns, but the campaign didn't take as well in high-spirited Joplin. "Attendance at the temperance meeting last night at the Presbyterian Church was rather small," reported the *Daily Herald* in early January, a time during which similar meetings in neighboring towns were drawing large crowds. The next day, the representative of the Murphy Movement who had helped conduct the meeting received "an urgent call" to go to Columbus, Kansas, and initiate the movement there. He left almost immediately and presumably received a more enthusiastic reception in Columbus than he had in Joplin.

Over a decade after the Carthage newspaperman had lampooned Joplin for the "calamity" of allowing itself to run out of beer, the town was still noted for its dissipated ways, but its citizens sometimes turned the tables, making fun of the stuffy morality of neighboring communities. In August 1890, for instance, a *Joplin Sunday Herald* reporter recounted the story of two men from "the marvelously quiet state of Kansas" who paid a visit to Joplin the previous Saturday to "see the sights" of the bustling town. Kansas had passed a prohibition law several years earlier, and back home the men were firm advocates of "the dry cause." However, after spending a few hours in Joplin and discussing at length the propriety of "taking a smile or so," the "pair of sunflower products" decided they couldn't visit the raucous town without laying aside their scruples "to the extent of imbibing a modicum of beer."

The *Sunday Herald* reporter then finished the story of what happened after "the advocates of prohibition from prohibition Kansas" let down their guard:

> *Once let a Kansan, who drinks at all, arrive at a place where stimulants are available, and he's certain to wind up as drunk as a "biled owl," regardless of whether his initial drink is beer, ale, porter or soda. The Kansans of this sketch were no exceptions.*
>
> *They beered up, ginned up and whiskied up until they didn't know whether they were afoot or horseback. They visited every house of vile repute in the city; swore like sea pirates and sang snatches of*

Little Annie Rooney until people for blocks around were terribly fatigued. They insisted upon scrapping with every one whom they met, and had they not fallen into the hands of a good samaritan, the law's octopus would have gathered them in and their families in Kansas, where no one ever imbibes, would have suffered disgrace.

Another thirteen years down the road, Joplin was still a drinking man's town, and local authorities were still struggling to enforce the liquor laws. After a jail trusty, who was sent on an errand on Sunday, October 11, 1903, came back drunk, the police department spent the next few days, according to the *Joplin Globe*, "making a strenuous effort to find out where whisky and other liquors are being sold on Sunday" and trying to determine "why so many men are arrested for drunkenness on the Sabbath."

In 1909, evangelist Billy Sunday held a revival in Joplin, emboldening temperance advocates to seek a local option referendum to make the city dry. Despite a hard-fought campaign by "professional prohibitionists," Joplin voters defeated the question early the following year by a 56 percent majority. (At about the same time, the neighboring communities of Carthage, Webb City, and Carterville went dry under local option referendums.) The handwriting, however, was on the wall. Even the *Joplin Globe*, which had editorialized against the local option, agreed that fifty-four saloons in Joplin was "a ridiculous number" for a town of its size. (Joplin's population had more than tripled since 1880 and stood at about thirty-two thousand in 1910.) The *Globe* also asserted that there were too many saloons in town that defied the Sunday closing law, stayed open beyond the stipulated hour on other days, maintained "so-called winerooms," and "acted as a sort of appointment to gambling houses."

The temperance movement finally succeeded, of course, in making prohibition the law of the land in 1919 under the Eighteenth Amendment to the Constitution. The law was scheduled to take effect at the stroke of midnight on July 1, and "wet" Joplin was a frenzy of activity in the days leading up to the deadline. People from miles around who lived in "dry" territories trekked to Joplin to stock up on John Barleycorn, and record sales were reported. (The Prohibition act initially outlawed the sale but not the possession of alcoholic drinks.)

On the eve of the law's taking effect, Joplinites marked the occasion with wild revelry. All the saloons were jammed throughout the evening, as were all the cafés that served alcohol. "No New Year's party in the history of Joplin... could be compared with it," said the *Joplin Globe* the next day. "When midnight approached the merrymakers were well along toward that state where every one is a 'jolly good fellow.'" When the fateful hour arrived, women jumped onto tables and starting singing "How Dry I Am" and similar ditties, while out in the streets "the revelry was nearly as bad. Men and boys paraded Main street shouting and yelling," and both men and women in automobiles drove up and down the street screaming and shouting out the open windows. The Joplin police arrested seventy-eight people for drunkenness, even though, reported the *Globe* on July 1, they limited their arrests to those "who had become so intoxicated they will not realize until late today they were guests of the city."

Joplin had forty-nine "thirst parlors" before Prohibition took effect, but only six remained open after July 1. Even though the law's initial provisions allowed the sale of "kickless beer" and other drinks containing no more than two and three quarters percent alcohol, the saloonkeepers said that, with whiskey barred, they could not make enough money to pay expenses.

Thus did Prohibition bring Joplin's long love affair with liquor to a hiatus. After the law was repealed in 1933, Joplin once again soon developed a reputation as a party town. The bars of Joplin did an especially lively business during World War II, when soldiers from nearby Camp Crowder would flock to town on weekend passes, but by the middle of the twentieth century the town had been infiltrated by too many cultivating influences to ever again surrender to Bacchus without reserve as it had during the reckless days of its youth.

TWISTING THE TIGER'S TAIL

Main Street presented its old-time appearance last night. The gambling halls
and saloons were crowded and money seems to be plenty.
—Joplin Herald, *quoted in the* Springfield Times, *March 6, 1878*

When those of us who live in the Midwest think of booming mining towns and lively cow towns of the Old West, images from classic TV shows such as *Bonanza* and *Gunsmoke* likely come to mind. We might think of dance hall girls and high-dollar gamblers frequenting the saloons of Virginia City or Dodge City. What many of us may not stop to consider, however, is that in the early 1870s, southwest Missouri was still very much a part of the Wild West, and the booming mining town of Joplin, like its lively counterparts in Kansas and Nevada, drew many adventurers and ne'er-do-wells, including more than its share of gamblers. As the *Joplin Daily Herald* observed in 1879, "Joplin has a great many of the sporting fraternity."

Gambling was prevalent in Joplin almost from the town's founding, and any attempt to control it during the very early days was left mostly to county officials headquartered twenty miles away in Carthage. In the fall of 1873, for instance, the Jasper County sheriff and two of his deputies, acting on a judge's order, trekked from the county seat to raid several of Joplin's gambling houses and seize all the gambling tables and apparatus they could find. Like the rest of the nation, Joplin was still recovering from the great economic panic of 1873, and even the gambling business had temporarily slacked off. So, the raid was not as successful as it might have been, and the officers brought back to

Carthage only a taro and roulette wheel and a keno outfit, which were to be destroyed by fire. "Owing to the hard times," explained the *Carthage Weekly Banner*, "not more than two or three of these houses were open, or else enough gambling furniture could have been seized to make a good sized bonfire."

In Joplin, as elsewhere, gambling and drinking tended to go hand in hand. There might have been a few gambling operations that were located in buildings completely separate from any saloon and that had no business connection to any saloon, but in most cases the gambling rooms adjoined the saloons. The saloonkeepers themselves occasionally kept a gambling device or staged a gambling game in the main barroom. More often, though, gambling was carried on by others in an adjacent room set aside for that purpose, and the saloonkeeper was only indirectly involved in the operation, if at all. For instance, saloonkeepers Gottlieb Schmierer and Henry Sapp were each cited in June 1880 for leasing a building for gambling (Sapp's property presumably being the rooms over the Miner's Drift), but there's no evidence that either man ran a gambling operation himself.

Some of the games played at the gambling houses were hazard (a dice game from which craps developed), keno, poker, and roulette, but by far the most popular game in Joplin and the Old West in general was faro.

An 1890s Old West faro game. *Courtesy of Legends of America.*

Faro can be played by laying out thirteen cards of a single suit (usually spades) from one deck of cards, arranged face up from ace to king, and then using a second deck to play the game. However, faro tables used in saloons and gambling establishments already had the layout pasted or painted on the surface. Players, often called punters, bought chips (usually called "checks") from the person running the game. This person was called the banker and was usually the owner of the gambling establishment or his designee (e.g. the dealer). Thus, "faro bank" could refer to the stakes in a game of faro, the gambling house where the game was held, or the game itself.

When the game was ready to begin, a deck of cards was placed in a device called a faro box, which had a slit at the top that would only allow the cards to be dealt one at a time from the top. The dealer burned the top card of the deck and then dealt the next two cards face up. If the card a player had bet on matched the first card turned up (called the banker's card), the player lost, and the dealer or banker collected the player's bet. If the card a player had bet on matched the second card turned up (called the player's card), the player won, and the banker paid the player double his bet (i.e. returned the bet and gave him an equal amount as winnings). If neither of the two cards turned up matched the card a player had bet on, he could retrieve his bet or let it ride for the next two-card turn. The layout also contained a "high card" space that allowed players the added option of betting that the player's card would be higher than the banker's.

If the two cards turned up were a pair, the banker collected half of all bets placed on that card. For instance, if both cards were jacks, the banker got half of all bets placed on the jack. This constituted the house's only advantage if the game was fair. The narrow odds in favor of the bank were, therefore, one of the main attractions of faro, but many faro boxes were rigged to ensure the house a better take.

Faro was commonly called "bucking the tiger" or "twisting the tiger's tail," sobriquets that were thought to have derived from the fact that the backs of early playing cards sometimes had drawings of Bengal tigers. A city or a street where faro thrived might be called "Tiger Town" or "Tiger Alley."

Two of the more notorious gamblers of early Joplin were James "Bud" Fagg and his older brother, J.P. "Pink" Fagg. The Faggs grew up in the raucous atmosphere of Civil War Springfield, where their father was a storekeeper who often ran afoul of the law for minor violations like selling liquor without a license, maintaining a gambling operation, and similar offenses. Bud Fagg drifted to the booming mining town of Joplin during the mid-1870s, when he was about twenty-two years old. Pink Fagg had already spent a hitch in the Missouri State Penitentiary for robbery by the time he joined his brother in late 1877.

Bud Fagg's first scrape with the law in Joplin came in December 1877 when he was cited in circuit court for betting on faro. He was again indicted for betting on faro in the spring of 1879 and then again in December of the same year. Pink Fagg, who was a less frequent offender in Jasper County than Bud only because he was more transient and spent less time in Joplin than his brother, was also charged with betting on faro in December 1879. Pink did not get in trouble in the county again until he tried to kill his wife at Carthage in September 1881. He had reportedly taken his bride out of a Joplin whorehouse and told her if he ever caught her in such a place again, he would kill her. When she deserted him and took up residence in a questionable resort at Carthage, Pink trekked to the county seat to try to make good on his threat, but she recovered from the gunshot wound he inflicted. Pink later shot and wounded a man at Pierce City, a crime for which he spent a second stint at Jeff City, and still later he killed a man at Fort Smith, Arkansas. Bud Fagg, meanwhile, continued to haunt the dives of Joplin and got in trouble for gambling several more times. In the spring of 1880, he reportedly lost $300 at the faro table in a single day—Saturday, April 17. It didn't stop him from indulging his passion, though. Later the same year, he was again charged with betting on faro, paid a $10 fine, and went back to his sport. He was still hanging around Joplin in 1881 when he was called to testify as a witness in a case of selling liquor on Sunday against Henry Sapp.

Besides the Fagg brothers, other notorious gamblers of early Joplin included Jake Pecora and several men known only by colorful nicknames like Boston Joe, Chicago Jack, Dutch Charley, and Springfield Red.

Periodically, local authorities made a token effort to crack down on gambling just as they occasionally made a nominal effort to enforce the liquor laws. For instance, the city passed a new ordinance against gambling in the spring of 1879, and on May 3 Marshal Hamilton raided the gambling houses at about ten o'clock in the morning. He "caught several of the boys" in the act, according to the *Daily Herald*, and told them they had "better turn their boxes over." At the Port Royal Saloon, Chicago Jack was dealing faro to a large group and had several dollars' worth of chips out. Hamilton made him "'shut up shop' and cash the ivories," leaving him fifty dollars behind for the morning. The next day, the *Herald* reported the raid under the heading "The Tiger Throttled," but the editor wasn't convinced that the so-called crackdown would have any long-term effect in diminishing gambling in Joplin. "Similar ordinances have been passed and attempts made to enforce them heretofore," he observed, "but all such attempts have been futile, and it is thought by many that this is only the regular periodical streak of morality and will soon give way."

Early Joplinites, of course, didn't have to go to the gambling houses to gamble. They tended to bet on almost anything and everything, whether it be a cockfight, a horse race, or a foot race. Betting on horse races was especially popular. A straight, half-mile racetrack was built in the early 1870s running diagonally from near the entrance of the city cemetery (i.e. Fairview) to near the current site of West Central Elementary School. In June 1874, a big horse race was held at the track between a Joplin horse named Daisy and a horse from Stockton. About two thousand spectators attended the event, Daisy won the race, and an estimated $5,000 changed hands. Later the same year, Daisy lost to a mare from Seneca, and some of the people in the large crowd, reported the *Carthage Weekly Banner*, had "bet their money, boots, and everything else on the Joplin nag."

Billiards was another popular game for betting. In May 1879, Henry Sapp hosted a big tournament with a $400 purse at the Miner's Drift. Entrants in the contest were limited to three accomplished, local billiard players, with the winner to receive $200 and the other two to get $100 apiece. The game sparked a lot of interest among the sporting class of Joplin, and a large amount of money changed hands on the "outside" in addition to the distribution of the purse to the participants.

Gambling rooms persisted in Joplin into the twentieth century, but Prohibition, in addition to shutting down the saloons, effectively closed the gambling establishments. The few gambling operations that remained were driven even further underground than they already were. Today, except for the state lottery, games of chance are still illegal in southwest Missouri, and gambling in Joplin is limited mainly to purchasing a Jokers Wild ticket at the corner store, informal betting among friends, or playing a Friday night poker game at a buddy's house. The gambling houses of yesteryear are long gone; then again, they're not necessary, since the casinos of northeast Oklahoma, where most forms of gambling are legal, are only a short drive away.

RAISING HELL GENERALLY

The latest event within its walls, and one, we think, that will cap the climax anywhere, was a pig race for a prize, which took place last Friday night.
—Springfield Times, *February 27, 1878, commenting on the diverse and unseemly uses of the Tabernacle, one of the primary places of worship in early-day Joplin*

From hearing tales about Joplin's early years—or, indeed, from reading the previous chapters of this book—one might get the idea that nearly every man in town was a drunk, a whoremonger, an inveterate gambler, or some combination thereof. Such a stereotype would, of course, be false. There were many upstanding citizens even during Joplin's earliest days, and not all amusements involved liquor, games of chance, or women of easy virtue. Most of the folks who were not directly involved in the town's vice, however, still knew how to have a good time, as early Joplinites indulged in their fair share of sheer merrymaking and what the *Daily Herald* called "raising hell generally."

Sometimes the hell-raising turned violent, of course, but often it was little more than entertainment. In the spring of 1875, for instance, two Joplin men who had been involved in a running dispute for some time decided to settle the argument through a fistfight to be held at a designated time and place. On Sunday, May 16, "the two pugilistic individuals," as the *Carthage Weekly Banner* called them, went across the line into Newton County, "accompanied by about 200 spectators," and made preparations for a more or less formal boxing match. A ring was laid out on the ground, the rules were discussed, and seconds were even chosen. Then "the combatants went at it," continued the *Banner*. "Several blows were exchanged, when a misunderstanding arose in regard to the rules of the battle. Both parties seemed anxious enough to quit, and the fight resulted in a draw."

Although the number of fistfights and the amount of gunplay in rowdy Joplin were disproportionate to the population, most diversions were of a tamer variety, and just as they do today, citizens sometimes sought relaxation rather than excitement during their leisure time. Grand Falls south of town on Shoal Creek was a popular resort for townspeople almost from Joplin's inception, and citizens, particularly those who did not frequent the beer gardens on Turkey Creek, often retired to the vicinity of the falls to fish, swim, or just get away from town for a while. The community celebrated its very first Fourth of July at the falls in 1872 with a big picnic during the day. Activities included orations and band music followed by a fireworks display when nighttime rolled around.

Dancing was also a popular pastime in early Joplin. The saloons sometimes doubled as dance halls featuring what Shaner, in his *Story of Joplin*, called a "rough sort of dancing," and the booming mining camp of Lone Elm at the north edge of Joplin reportedly sported three "dancing clubs" by itself in the spring of 1877. However, dancing that even Shaner would not have considered coarse or raunchy was also common. The Opera House and other gathering places often hosted more formal dances like the New Year's Eve masquerade ball at the Berz Hall at Fourth and Main that ushered in 1878.

Sketch of an 1880s dance hall from the *National Police Gazette*.

Raising Hell Generally

Not only was Joplin's first divine service held in a saloon, but also, conversely, one of its early houses of worship was often given over to secular uses that some observers found just as unseemly as holding church in a barroom. The Tabernacle, built at the southwest corner of Fourth and Virginia in 1876, functioned almost like a town hall and played host to numerous public gatherings, some of them offered for pure entertainment.

When a roller-skating craze hit Joplin in late 1877, the Tabernacle served as the skating rink. Chairs were taken outside to make room for the skating and then carried back inside for Sunday services, and half the money taken in at the rink was contributed to the church. Large groups of "Holy Rollers," as the skaters were sometimes called, gathered at the Tabernacle each night throughout the final week of 1877 to participate in their newfound recreation. One evening, according to the *Daily Herald*, "the amusement was kept up until quite late and though a number were present who had experienced many a fall, and had finally become adepts, yet there were those present who contributed largely by their indiscriminate tumbling and kept the audience in an uproar of good humor." Prominent among the skaters was Marshal Hamilton, who, commented the *Herald*, had managed "by systematic practice" to acquire "sufficient skill to keep his center of gravity."

The skill level of the skaters had improved enough by the following week that contests to decide the most graceful female skater and the most graceful male skater were held on January 3, 1878, and prizes awarded. As a jest, a third competition was also staged to pick the "the ugliest man on wheels," and the prize was "carried off by our jolly, good-natured marshal, Cass Hamilton."

Such mixing of religion and merrymaking as that which characterized the goings-on at the Tabernacle earned Joplin frequent criticism from its neighbors and only enhanced its reputation as an evil and irreverent place. In early January 1880, for instance, the editor of the *Neosho Miner and Mechanic* waxed indignant over the indecorous fundraising activities of a Joplin congregation that hoped to build a new church. Calling Joplin "a queer place," the editor continued:

The ladies belonging to the church are working with vim. During the holidays they had a festival, at which there was music and dancing, and several articles of value were raffled off, the whole thing realizing about one hundred dollars for the cause of religion. To-night they give a grand leap year ball, at which a magnificent diamond ring is to be drawn, lottery fashion. Some of the most prominent lady members of the church are floor managers, and doubtless they will waltz a good amount of money out of those who attend. We presume the minister will be the beau of the ball, and all the ladies will vie with each other as to who shall have the honor of dancing with him. Thus do Christians in Joplin renounce the devil and all his works, and the vain pomp and glory of this world.

Joplinites, though, did not meekly abide such criticism. Responding to the report in the *Miner and Mechanic*, the editor of the *Daily Herald* accused his counterpart at Neosho of being "pious and sanctimonious."

For several years during Joplin's early days, the town, in celebration of its mining heritage, observed Mardi Gras with a gala day dedicated to Rex Plumbum, a fictional personification of lead. The day started with a big parade through downtown, featuring masked marchers and horsemen arrayed in extravagant costumes and the character of Rex Plumbum serving as grand marshal, while thousands of spectators, some of them decked out in costumes as well, crowded around. The first annual event, held on February 25, 1880, was described in the next day's *Joplin Daily Herald*:

A full brass band rigged out in the most curious and original costumes headed the procession, and then came His Royal Highness Rex Plumbum, mounted on a donkey not much larger than a jack rabbit. The King wore a gorgeous costume, and wore a glittering crown of sheet lead...The streets were crowded with people, and everyone seemed in the best of humor. There seemed to be a general understanding that the Mardi Gras was gotten up especially for a good time, and they carried it out to the fullest extent.

The daytime festivities finally broke off about dark near the Opera House, where the celebrants gathered for a masquerade ball. "In a short time the hall was crowded with merry dancers," said the *Herald*, "and it was almost daylight before they dispersed."

Twenty years later, at the turn of the twentieth century, Joplinites still enjoyed a festive occasion. During late October 1899, downtown Joplin hosted a street fair lasting several days and culminating on Saturday night. According to the *Sunday Herald*, the event "wound up last night in one grand uproarious and spontaneous blaze of fun...The streets were never so crowded before and the confetti man and the rubber ball man, from the business done, must be millionaires this morning." The reporter claimed there was "very little disorder" at the carnival but admitted that about twenty arrests "of young men

R 29, 1899.--SUNDAY MORNI

TOWN WAS WILD.

Street Fair Ends in Hilarity.

Which Grew a Little Rough at Times.

Barrelfuls of Rice and Confetti.

Thrown, But No Serious Disturbances.

A headline from the *Joplin Daily Herald* proclaims the atmosphere of revelry that characterized an 1890s street fair in Joplin.

who became too noisy" were made. He also allowed that the crowd at one point "became so demonstrative that the policemen thought it necessary to wave their revolvers."

Joplinites didn't need a special occasion, though, to turn Saturday night into a jubilee. From its very beginning, Joplin was what Shaner called "a Saturday night town." Miners, store clerks, and other employees all got paid on Saturday, and most of them were itching to spend some of their hard-earned money. All the businesses stayed open late on Saturday night, and people flocked to the downtown district from the rest of the city and from outlying areas to partake in the carnival. According to Shaner, there was occasional roughhousing in some of the saloons and "sometimes a street fight," but serious violence was rare.

When Shaner wrote *The Story of Joplin* in 1948, the town was "still a busy place on Saturday night," according to the author. Indeed, there are still citizens living in Joplin today who recall when the downtown area was the place to be on Saturday night. For instance, Bunny Newton, senior owner of Newton's Jewelers located at the corner of Fifth and Main since 1939, told me a couple of years ago that he recalled when the downtown sidewalks were so crowded on Saturday nights that he had to take to the streets to get from one building to another. Downtown Joplin continued to hop on Saturday nights well into the 1950s, until new shopping centers and activities in other parts of town gradually drew people elsewhere. Although the downtown area, through revitalization efforts, has witnessed a comeback of sorts in recent years, the time when Main Street staged a spontaneous carnival at the end of each week has long since been consigned to history, like the extravagant masked processions that Rex Plumbum led over one hundred years ago.

THE BOSS BEER MAN AND OTHER FOUNDING FATHERS

*Cox did not deny it, and said that if any woman would rub their belly up
against him, he, Cox, would accommodate them.*
*—James N. Langley, testifying in an 1850s Greene County lawsuit that he
had told John C. Cox that the reason Cox lost his 1856 bid for reelection as
Jasper County surveyor was that he was "too handy with his cock"*

When present-day citizens of Joplin hear or read names like John C. Cox,
Charles Schifferdecker, Patrick Murphy, and Thomas Connor, we
think of men who gave the town its start—men who donated land for parks
and men who had streets and buildings named after them. We don't think of
such men as lawbreakers. Yet it's not surprising, given that Joplin was a place
where nearly everything was allowed, that even many of the town's founding
fathers got caught up in the vice. While most of Cox's shenanigans apparently
predated the town's incorporation, those of the other three men did not.

Patrick Murphy was born in Ireland in 1839 and came to Pennsylvania
with his parents as a ten-year-old lad. When he was twenty, he went west
and prospected for lead in Colorado for several months before entering
the freighting business with headquarters in Nebraska. In 1866, he came
to Carthage and went into the mercantile business. In 1871, when lead was
discovered along Joplin Creek, he moved to the area and laid out the town of
Murphysburg. He opened a store at the corner of First and Main, then went
into mining, and later had various other business interests, including banking.
After briefly detailing Murphy's contribution to early Joplin, F.A. North, in

Sketch of Patrick Murphy from North's *History of Jasper County*.

his 1883 *History of Jasper County*, added by way of summary, "In fact few enterprises of considerable importance have ever been carried to a successful completion in Joplin without Patrick Murphy at the helm."

Although Murphy's involvement in Joplin's early-day vice was marginal, drinking and gambling were so pervasive that it would have been difficult for anyone, especially someone of Murphy's prominence, to have had nothing whatsoever to do with either activity. For example, while there is no evidence that Murphy was an ardent gambler himself, it is interesting to note that he was indicted at least twice in Jasper County Circuit Court for leasing buildings to other men for gambling purposes, once in June 1878 and again in December of the same year. Similarly, there is no reason to believe that Murphy was a hard drinker, but neither did he shy away from saloons. In the spring of 1877, for instance, after lead was discovered across the Kansas state line on Short Creek, he helped start the town of Empire City, and later in the year he took a tour of neighboring Galena's notorious "Red Hot Street," where, according to the *Galena Miner*, he "set up one hundred and forty drinks in one saloon" and visited several others.

Like Murphy, Thomas Connor was an Irishman who came to Joplin during its very early days. From the mid-'70s until at least the early '80s, Connor operated the Senate Saloon on Main Street of East Joplin.

Because of the nature of his business, it's not surprising that he was more directly involved in the vice of early Joplin than Murphy. In March 1875, Connor was charged in circuit court with permitting a gambling device to be used on his premises, and in September of the same year he was indicted for "keeping a gambling house" and took a forfeiture of bond as a fine. Like most of the early-day saloons in Joplin, the Senate didn't always abide by the Sunday closing ordinance, and Connor was cited for the offense on more than one occasion. At the time of the 1880 census, the thirty-two-year-old Connor and his wife, Melissa, were living in East Town, and his occupation was listed as "saloonkeeper."

Connor, like many Joplin businessmen, also had mining interests. A fleet runner, he reportedly grubstaked himself with money he won in foot races. At any rate, his mining investments eventually enabled him to outgrow the Senate, and in 1881 he purchased a half interest in the Joplin Hotel. (About the same time, Warren Murphy, no apparent relation to Patrick Murphy, took over operation of the Senate Saloon.) Eventually, Connor became a wealthy banker and capitalist, and according to legend, he was Joplin's first millionaire. In 1906 and 1907, he built the renowned Connor Hotel, where the Joplin Hotel had stood at the corner of Fourth and Main, and the Connor remained a fixture in downtown Joplin until it collapsed during demolition in 1978.

Born in Germany in 1851, Charles Schifferdecker came to America in 1869 at the age of eighteen and soon migrated west. After working briefly in breweries at Quincy, Illinois, and St. Louis, Missouri, near the beginning of 1875 he landed at Baxter Springs, Kansas, where he continued in the brewery business, working this time for Edward Zelleken. In October of the same year, he moved to Joplin, where he and Zelleken started a wholesale beer and ice business. Zelleken continued living in Baxter Springs until late 1881, leaving day-to-day operations of the Joplin business to Schifferdecker.

Schifferdecker lived initially on Turkey Creek near the Rothanbarger home that is still standing today. In early 1876, he opened a beer garden near his home about a quarter of a mile east of Castle Rock. The garden served as a popular gathering spot and resort for Joplinites for several years. The beer garden included a dance hall, but in November 1878, the *Daily Herald* reported that Schifferdecker was converting the dance hall to an icehouse. "He proposes," the reporter commented, "to keep Joplinites from 'boiling over' next summer." In early August 1879, Schifferdecker entertained a large party at the garden and, according to the *Herald*, was named the "boss beer man" by the people in attendance.

The beer business boomed in thirsty Joplin, and Schifferdecker's enterprises thrived. His beer garden remained popular, and his wholesale distributing company, which became the franchised Anheuser dealer in the Joplin area, also prospered. For instance, on April 30, 1880, the eve of Joplin's celebrated Bock Beer Day, Schifferdecker was kept busy delivering bock beer by the keg to the town's drinking establishments in anticipation of a booming saloon business the next day. At some point, Schifferdecker started his own brewery, and like so many early Joplin businessmen, he also had mining interests that helped make him wealthy.

Not only prominent, Schifferdecker was also a well-liked citizen of early Joplin, and it's not hard to see why. His good name was no doubt due, at least in part, to his generosity with his products. For instance, in the summer of 1879, Schifferdecker and saloonkeeper Henry Willhardt treated the workers at the Black Darling mine to a free keg of Lemp's beer. In March 1881, the *Daily Herald* reported that Schifferdecker was supplying his customers with ice free of charge, and the newspaper dubbed him the "boss brewery man." A month later, Schifferdecker gave a free keg of beer to a Frisco Railroad crew. At Christmas 1881, he gave a free keg of beer to each of the customers of his wholesale business. (An incident that seems amusing now but probably wasn't at the time also occurred in 1881 while Schifferdecker was making his rounds in his new beer wagon. His team was standing outside the Johnsons' saloon at the Vaudeville, while he was presumably making a delivery inside, when the horses became spooked and ran away, charging up the Broadway hill into East Town before finally halting when they ran into a hitching rail in front of John Roesch's saloon on Main Street.)

Just as it's easy to imagine that Schifferdecker's liberality with his beer may have contributed to his popularity with the people of early Joplin, it's also not unexpected that the nature of his business occasionally put him at cross swords with the law. For instance, on successive weeks in late May and early June 1877, Schifferdecker was cited for selling liquor on Sunday, and in June 1878, he was charged with the same offense. In December 1878, he was again indicted for selling liquor on Sunday, pled guilty, and paid a five-dollar fine. Most, if not all, of these charges no doubt stemmed from Schifferdecker's operation of his beer garden, which was mainly a weekend attraction.

In 1888, Schifferdecker got out of the beer business but continued and expanded his other enterprises. For instance, he helped organize the First National Bank of Joplin and served as its president for a number of years.

Home built by Charles Schifferdecker at Fifth and Sergeant in Joplin as it appears today.

Today, the "boss beer man," because of his generous donations to the city of Joplin during his later years, is remembered principally as the man who lent his name to Schifferdecker Park, one of the town's main recreation facilities, and Schifferdecker Avenue, one of the city's main thoroughfares. The mansion he built in 1890 at the corner of Fifth and Sergeant is also still standing.

Although William Swindle was not someone we normally think of as a founding father of Joplin, he was important enough that a neighborhood of the early-day town, Swindle Hill, was named after him, and he was involved in a peculiar incident that makes him an interesting subject for this book. On July 11, 1874, C.E. Combs, a constable of Galena Township, called at Swindle's store and home on Swindle Hill (near the present-day intersection of Seventh and Murphy Boulevard) to serve a fee bill in the amount of $4.90 issued by justice of the peace Ira Creech. Combs went first to the store and was told that Swindle was home sick. He then started on horseback toward the house and met Swindle coming toward the store. When he told Swindle the purpose of his call, Swindle claimed he didn't owe the debt because he had already paid it to a different justice. Combs said he hadn't and accused Swindle of dishonesty. The argument escalated from there, and when Combs cursed Swindle and called him a scoundrel, Swindle picked up a stick about five feet long and an inch and half thick and hit Combs with it. Combs, who later filed an assault charge against Swindle, claimed he was beat repeatedly with the stick, but Swindle said he merely tapped Combs a time or two with it to get across the message that he *would* beat him if Combs didn't leave him alone. Swindle said the constable then turned his horse around and left. In a strange twist, Justice Creech was initially scheduled to hear the assault charge against Swindle. However, the defendant was granted a change of venue to a different justice, and the final outcome of the case is unknown.

About a year after the incident, though, Swindle moved back to his farm near Sarcoxie, where he had lived before coming to Joplin at the beginning of the lead boom. Later, he moved into Sarcoxie and engaged in the mercantile business.

FROM JAYHAWKER TO JOPLINITE

*Joplin had its visits from the James gang and the Younger brothers gang
of outlaws.*
—*Dolph Shaner,* The Story of Joplin

A number of adventurous men who had already made names for themselves during the Kansas-Missouri border conflict of the Civil War were drawn to the booming mining town of Joplin during the 1870s, and postwar outlaws like Jesse James also paid occasional visits to the wide-open town. Prominent among the former group were Charles R. "Doc" Jennison, John David Mefford, and C.F. "Fletch" Taylor. Although generally considered acceptable and even respectable citizens of Joplin, they were not untouched by the vice that permeated the town, and, in some cases, they readily embraced it.

A New York native, Jennison settled in free-soil Kansas in the late 1850s and quickly aligned himself with radical abolitionist leaders like James Montgomery in opposing proslavery settlers and border ruffians from Missouri. During the early stages of the Civil War, Jennison was made colonel of the Seventh Kansas Cavalry and led destructive raids into the Show-Me State, earning infamy for the regiment as "Jennison's jayhawkers." Later in the war, his heavy-handed tactics while serving as colonel of the Fifteenth Kansas Cavalry enhanced his notorious reputation. Many Southern-leaning Missourians viewed Jennison with the same contempt that Kansans held for such Missouri guerrilla leaders as William Quantrill, mastermind of the Lawrence massacre.

After the war, Jennison served two terms in the Kansas legislature and another term in the state senate before coming, in the late 1870s, to Joplin, where he opened a restaurant and saloon on Main Street. Like many early-day Joplin businessmen, Jennison also tried his hand at mining from time to time, but what he apparently enjoyed doing more than anything else was gambling.

In the rowdy atmosphere of Joplin's early days, where characters of every stripe were tolerated and even welcomed, Jennison played the role of a leading citizen and was viewed in that light by some Joplinites, but other observers (no doubt Southern sympathizers for the most part), saw him, at best, as a buffoon. For instance, when Jennison first made his appearance in the Joplin area about the spring of 1877, a Carthage newspaper served notice to its readers that "Jennison the Kansas jayhawker is mining in the Tracy lands near Webb City."

Mining, though, was too much like work for the portly Jennison, who spent most of his time hanging out in the saloons and gambling halls of Joplin. Sometime in 1877, he opened his own restaurant and saloon on Main Street and called it the Saratoga. In the fall of the same year, he developed a case of sore eyes, and he spent the next three months rambling around Joplin in blue goggles. To attract gamblers and, no doubt, to indulge his own penchant for games of chance, Colonel Jennison, as he was usually called, installed a faro bank at the Saratoga. In December, he was charged in circuit court with unlawfully setting up "a certain gambling device commonly called faro."

Jennison evidently prided himself on serving only quality food at his establishment. In early January 1878, he let it be known that he had a "fine lot of mackinaw trout" on the menu, and a couple of days later a notice in the *Daily Herald* assured readers that Colonel Jennison's fare was "warranted to contain neither feline nor canine scraps."

Like most Joplin saloons, the Saratoga occasionally served complimentary meals. When the editor of the *Daily Herald* was unable to attend a free repast on the evening of January 4, 1878, Jennison sent the newspaperman a venison ham anyway. "From this," the editor remarked the next day, "it will be seen that the Col. is extending his field of usefulness and charity. If people don't get time to attend his famous free suppers he will send the necessary articles for a square meal around. Vive la Jennison."

The old jayhawker enjoyed a good joke as well as the next fellow. On the evening of January 16, 1878, Jennison called some of the leading citizens of Joplin together at the Saratoga for an elaborate ceremony during which he presented city marshal Hamilton with a diamond pin and ring set as a prize for winning the "ugliest man" contest at the town's skating rink.

In late January, Jennison gave the editors of the *Joplin News* and the *Joplin Daily Herald* each a fur hat as a gift. His charity apparently extended beyond the dinner table, or else he was a public relations man ahead of his time looking to ensure favorable press coverage.

In early April 1878, Jennison, while still maintaining the Saratoga, opened another business called the Bon Ton. Although primarily a gambling establishment, the Bon Ton also served food. Soon after the place opened, the *Daily Herald* reported that "Col. Jennison is an epicure. He has the best or nothing. The coffee for the 'Bon Ton' is the celebrated Mocha, and he is the only purchaser in the city."

In late May, Jennison had a snow white mockingbird delivered to him from Florida, and the *Daily Herald* announced to its readers that they could stop by the Bon Ton to see the rare bird.

Given Jennison's history of fighting for the cause of abolition, it is not surprising to learn that he employed several black workers at the Bon Ton. In early June, it was reported that two of them would often break out in song while they worked, entertaining customers with old Negro spirituals.

In mid-June, Jennison closed the Bon Ton, but the reason was obviously not because he had tired of gambling. On June 11, 1878, about the time he closed the Bon Ton, Jennison spent the day gambling (and also bankrolling Bud Fagg) at a faro bank kept by Thomas V. Day at Lafayette Vancil's saloon, and the colonel won over $600. Day apparently felt he had been somehow cheated and tried unsuccessfully to convince Jennison to return his winnings. The next month, in a strange bit of irony, Day filed a replevin suit to try to get the money back, claiming it had been won fraudulently through illegal gambling. Because he feared that Jennison was getting ready to leave town, Day also filed a suit attaching Jennison's property, an action that required Day to put up a bond in case the property were damaged or lost. The case was finally settled a year later when Day dropped his suits and Jennison released Day of his obligation on the attachment bond.

Also in June 1878, Jennison was thrown from his buggy when his horse reared and tipped it over. Later in the year, he bought a new horse, a fast trotter, which he reportedly drove on the streets of Joplin every day.

Although Jennison had received medical training as a young man before coming west, he rarely practiced medicine. However, in December 1878 he attended saloonkeeper William Bassett when the man took ill.

About the same time, Jennison began fixing up a room in the rear of John Pabst's Port Royal Saloon. The purpose of fixing up the room is not known for sure, but it was probably used for gambling, because it is known that Jennison kept faro devices in two different establishments in early 1879, one at his pal William Bassett's place and a second one at another saloon that was not the Saratoga.

In March 1879, Jennison was sued by J.E. Thrasher, who sought the return of eighty-eight dollars he had lost at one of the faro banks. The court, however, decided against the plaintiff, ruling not only that he could take nothing from his suit but also that he must pay court costs. Also in March, Jennison and Ralph Muir opened what the *Daily Herald* called an "intelligence office" in the same building where Muir had his ice and wholesale beer business. Late the same month, Jennison went out to his mines, but he was soon back to doing what he liked best.

He was cited in circuit court for setting up a faro bank in June 1879 and again in August of the same year. Also in August, he, William Teets, and another man joined a gun club and tried their hands shooting at glass balls as target practice. The three men tied one another, reported the *Daily Herald*. "None of them hit a ball."

In late August, some of Jennison's friends began urging him to run for mayor of Joplin, and the *Daily Herald* opined that the colonel "would make a good mayor." He, however, was dissuaded from making the run or else lost the election, since it was later reported that his candidacy for city office was "disapproved."

In 1879, with an eye toward hosting a large exposition the following year, the City of Joplin laid out a fair grounds that included a racetrack in the southwest part of town (across present-day Maiden Lane from the Price Cutter supermarket), and Jennison, because of his interest in horse racing, was much involved in the project. In early September, when the grounds were nearing completion, Jennison took his gray mare out to the track for a trotting race against a horse owned by a man named Byler. "Quite a crowd," looked on, according to the *Daily Herald*, as Byler won and Jennison "failed to make a mile in four minutes."

Later in the month, Jennison gave some visiting dignitaries a tour of the exposition grounds, and still later in September he oversaw a series of races held at the track. "Col. Jennison deserves great credit for the admirable manner in which he conducted the races and managed the affair." It goes almost without saying, since Jennison was ram-rodding the event, that there was a lot of betting on the races.

In the spring of 1880, Jennison and some other men, including Fletch Taylor, took an interest in fishing and went out one day to the falls on Shoal Creek for an angling expedition. Jennison was the butt of jokes for several days afterward when he brought back only a small sunfish while most of the others caught good-sized bass.

A couple of days after a devastating tornado struck Marshfield, Missouri, on April 18, 1880, Jennison trekked to the Webster County town to assess the damage. Returning to Joplin, he addressed citizens at the Opera House who were interested in a Marshfield relief effort. Later in the month, the colonel made a trip to Eureka Springs, where, according to the *Carthage Daily Patriot*, he planned "to get rid of some of his 320 pounds of obesity." Perhaps the excursion to the healing waters helped him shed a few pounds, because later in the year, commenting on Jennison and another overweight man, the *Daily Herald* remarked that the combined weight of "the precious pair of infants is 494 pounds and 4 ounces."

On the evening of May 2, 1880, "Charley Jennison" fell down a flight of stairs, according to the *Daily Herald*, and "came down with a rush that would have done credit to a second rate cyclone. No damage, only a slight depression in the sidewalk where the top of his head was soothed to rest."

In early May, when the Joplin City Council ordered a crackdown on the gambling houses, Jennison wasted no time crossing the state line to the more hospitable environs of Kansas to pursue his pastime. He and his "reliable employee" Bud Fagg had gone on a gambling jaunt to neighboring Galena earlier in the year, and a day or two after his fall down the steps, Jennison, Fagg, and Boston Joe ventured across the border again.

A few days later, though, Jennison was back in Joplin, where he began transforming his clubrooms above the Miner's Drift Saloon into a reading room. (This was likely the same location where he had previously operated the Bon Ton.) Jennison planned to stock the room with classic literature for the free perusal of anyone who cared to "pass an hour in a pleasant and profitable manner," and he announced that no games of chance whatever would be permitted on the premises. Later in May, Jennison also reportedly rented the basement under the Golden Gate Saloon and planned to open it as a free soup kitchen. Skeptics like the editor of the *Neosho Miner and Mechanic*, however, viewed Jennison's sudden conversion with suspicion and rightly speculated that the "tiger" had not been killed in Joplin but only temporarily scotched.

Part of the reason, perhaps, that Jennison decided to swear off gambling (or at least swear off maintaining a gambling establishment himself) was that he knew what was facing him in the June term of circuit court. He was cited in at least seven separate cases for keeping a gambling device. He pleaded guilty and paid fines in two of the cases, while five others were continued until September after he posted bond.

Perhaps to avoid answering the remaining gambling charges against him, Jennison once again, in the summer of 1880, absconded to Galena, where he was reported to be "on his ear."

Evidently there weren't enough literati in early-day Joplin to sustain a reading room because by the time Jennison came back to town in the fall of 1880, he had had a change of heart about the best use of his rooms above Sapp's saloon and once again set up a gambling house there. In early October, he severely beat a customer over the head with a poker when the man entered the establishment and "endeavored to kick up a row."

A few months later, Jennison was back at Galena, where he and two other men got up a trotting race in the late spring of 1881 with two cases of beer and a bottle of liquor waged on the outcome. He also organized and took bets on several contests involving feats of physical strength, such as a match to see who could throw a baseball the farthest distance.

In addition, Jennison started working a mine, located near the town's only church, that was facetiously dubbed "the Jayhawker shaft." In June 1881, he and a partner were reported to have struck "big jack" at the mine. Apparently, however, by the time the brunt of summer rolled around, he once again had already tired of the hard work of mining. In July, the *Galena Miner* reported, "Jennison puts in his time now drinking lemonade and watching the thermometer. The buck rock has no attractions."

Jennison left the Joplin area sometime in the early 1880s and returned to Leavenworth, Kansas, where he had previously lived. He died there in 1884. Perhaps the greatly divided opinion that people in the Joplin area held of C.R. Jennison is best illustrated by the divergent comments with which area newspapers greeted the word of his death. The *Carthage Banner*, for instance, said that he "was a genial, whole-souled companion and...had a host of friends." The *Neosho Times*, on the other hand, claimed, "Jennison during the war was a thief" and that since the war he had been a professional gambler who had "lured more men to ruin than any man in the West. His disposition was overbearing and cruel and those who knew him best liked him least. The only regret that his death should call forth is that it did not occur long ago." The *Daily Herald* summed up the divided sentiment by remarking, "No man had as many bitter opponents and as many friends as Colonel C.R. Jennison."

John David Mefford was a captain (later a major) in the Sixth Kansas Cavalry during the Civil War. He fought at the First Battle of Newtonia in 1862 and various other engagements along the Missouri-Kansas border. He was captured in Arkansas during July 1864 and spent the remainder of the war in a Confederate prison.

He stayed in the army and lived at Leavenworth for several years after the war. He then came to Joplin in the mid-1870s and opened a saloon on Main Street. In March 1875, Mefford was charged in Jasper County Circuit Court records with permitting gambling in his house. The next month he was charged with betting on faro. In December 1877, he was again indicted, this time for keeping a "saloon, alehouse, or tippling shop open on Sunday."

Sometime in early 1878, Mefford's saloon became Vancil's saloon, where Jennison won the $600 playing at Day's faro bank later in the year. Closing his saloon gave Mefford time to pursue other pastimes, and in late February he and three other men went duck hunting on Center Creek.

Being a saloonkeeper, though, was more his line of work. Not long after turning his first saloon over to Vancil, Mefford bought or rented another place, which he was busy repairing and renovating during the month of May. When he opened the Sample Room at the end of the month, the *Daily Herald* proclaimed it "one of the coziest places in the city and a real beauty for a prescription clerk." (Mefford apparently had previously worked in a drugstore.) Less than a month after Mefford opened his new saloon, a new thirteen-pound boy appeared in the Mefford family from "baby land." The *Daily Herald* reported that the mother and child were doing fine and that "the father is improving."

In late December 1878, Mefford was again charged with selling liquor on Sunday. Not only did Mefford keep "extended" hours, but his Sample Room, like most Joplin drinking establishments, also occasionally served free meals to attract customers. The *Daily Herald* reported on February 1, 1879, that Major Mefford would "set a grand lunch tonight." In May of the same year, Mefford decided to take up mining, and he sold the stock and bar fixtures of the Sample Room to Herman Geldmacher.

In the summer of 1879, Mefford was working a shaft 125 feet deep, but like Jennison, he wasn't cut out for the hard-rock life. He soon relocated to Galena, and it was reported the following spring that his business there (probably a saloon) was still booming. Mefford later returned to Joplin and ran a saloon at 222 Main Street during the 1890s. He was still living in Joplin at the time of the 1900 census. He died shortly after the turn of the century and is buried at Fairview Cemetery.

Above: Mefford family plot at Joplin's Fairview Cemetery. John David Mefford's stone is the one in the foreground on the left.

Left, from left to right: Fletch Taylor, Frank James, and Jesse James, circa 1864. *Courtesy of the State Historical Society of Missouri-Columbia.*

C.F. "Fletch" Taylor was a leading citizen of early Joplin and was only marginally involved in the vice prevalent in the town, but he is an interesting subject for this book because of his close connection to Frank and Jesse James. During the Civil War, Taylor was a Quantrill lieutenant in the summer and fall of 1863, and the men under his immediate command included Frank James. The following year, he led his own guerrilla band, and both Frank and Jesse James served under him. He was seriously wounded in the summer of 1864 and had to have one of his arms amputated.

Fletch Taylor came to Joplin with his brother, John H. Taylor, in 1871, when the town was just getting started. John H. Taylor was one of Joplin's founding fathers and the man who carried the town's articles of incorporation to Jefferson City in the spring of 1873. He organized and served as president of the Joplin Mining and Smelting Company and later was also president of the Joplin Savings Bank. Fletch Taylor served with his brother as an officer in the Joplin Mining and Smelting Company and had other business interests as well. He was elected to the Joplin City Council in 1878. Previous authors have suggested that he also later served as a state legislator, although a historical listing of Missouri state representatives on the state archives' website does not confirm this assertion.

In December 1877, C.F. Taylor was indicted in Jasper County Circuit Court for betting on poker. This appears to have been his only brush with the law during his stay in Joplin, but his friendship with the James brothers was no doubt one of the primary reasons that the notorious outlaws made occasional stops in the area. Indeed, Shaner's *The Story of Joplin*, although it doesn't specifically name Fletch Taylor, says that, even though the James and Younger gangs paid visits to Joplin, they refrained from committing crimes while in the area "on account of friends, former members of the Quantrill guerrillas, who lived in Joplin and the district."

Stories abound in the local lore of the James brothers' connection to Joplin, and no doubt some of them are at least partially true. Shaner, for instance, tells the story of a would-be holdup of John Taylor's Joplin Savings Bank. Several men walked into the bank with the intent of robbing the place, but Fletch showed up and recognized some of the bandits, including Jesse James. Fletch invited the gang into a back office to meet his brother, and Jesse ordered his men to holster their guns. Later, Fletch had dinner with his old friends and visited the saloons and clubs of Joplin, where Jesse and pals were introduced under assumed names. Shaner also says that on another occasion Fletch Taylor ate supper in Joplin with the infamous Younger brothers.

While many of the tales about the James boys and other desperadoes making themselves at home in Joplin are merely legendary, the James brothers' connection to the area can be at least partially substantiated by contemporary sources. For instance, one local yarn tells of a time when the gang holed up in a hideout west of Joplin near present-day Belle Center, and records show that Fletch Taylor owned a large farm in that area. It seems plausible to conclude that the brothers may have been hiding out on their old friend's land. (Fletch also owned a home on Galena Avenue in East Joplin, but at the time of the 1880 census, the thirty-seven-year-old Taylor was living on Pearl Street with the family of saloonkeeper Henry Willhardt, his wife's stepfather.) Also, the *Daily Herald* reported in early June 1878 that Maggie James, sister to Frank and Jesse, had paid a visit to Fletch Taylor in Joplin, and on August 19, 1881, the same newspaper reported that a man who knew Jesse James claimed to have seen him on the streets of Joplin the previous day.

In addition, primary sources suggest that the infamous Younger gang had at least a peripheral connection to Joplin. While it is not known for sure that brothers Cole, Jim, and Bob spent any considerable time in the area, their half uncle Bruce Younger did abide in Joplin during the winter of 1875–76, as did Younger gang members Bill Chadwell, Charlie Pitts, and Hobbs Kerry.

In the spring of 1880, Fletch Taylor went to Colorado, but he returned to Joplin in September 1881. Later, Taylor moved to Nebraska and then to California, where he died in 1912.

A.S. AND CORA JOHNSON
AND THE VAUDEVILLE
VARIETY THEATRE

A Joplin theatrical company has a play on the boards entitled "Ten Bar Rooms in One Night, or the Johnson Movement." Joplin needs spanking.
—Springfield Times, *March 13, 1878, at the height of the temperance Murphy Movement that swept the Ozarks*

Augustus "A.S." Johnson and his wife, Cora, arrived in Joplin about 1872 or 1873. Johnson opened a vaudeville variety show in a building on Broadway, sometimes called the Star Concert Hall, and he and Cora also ran an adjoining saloon. The Vaudeville Theatre building had rooms to house the itinerant players while they were in town, and Cora also kept a stable of prostitutes on the premises at least part time.

Shaner's *Story of Joplin* paints a vivid and telling picture of Johnson's variety show:

> *This amusement hall provided a cheap vaudeville show of song and dance numbers. Occasionally a burlesque troupe from St. Louis acted before the brilliant kerosene floodlights, replaced later with more brilliant gas jets; burnt cork artists, Indian club swingers, slack rope walkers, banjo pickers and German bands entertained. It was a bad place for decent people, because many women who frequented the vaudeville reddened their cheeks with rouge and penciled their eye brows. They were even seen there in red petticoats*

or red scarfs, or red basques. It was a "sure sign" if a woman wore bright red in public in the seventies or eighties. As if this were not enough, the "hussies" on the stage, in the amusement emporium, were bold enough to appear in knee length skirts and whirled about showing a glimpse of lace on white muslin undergarments.

In January 1875, Cora Johnson was indicted in Jasper County Circuit Court on a charge of keeping a bawdyhouse, and she paid a $25 fine. When she was arrested in the fall of 1876 for the same offense and also for selling liquor without a license, she was released on a $300 bond put up by her husband and another man, and she was ordered to appear at the next term of court. Her hearing came up in March 1877, and the list of witnesses slated to testify in the case included Mollie Thomas, Josie Bauer, Georgia Price, and Anna Thatcher. These were the same four girls who were also called during the same term of court to testify as witnesses in cases of keeping a bawdyhouse against both Mollie Fisher and Mollie Tate. (It is known that at least one of the Mollies had her headquarters on Broadway very near the Vaudeville Theatre, and it is likely that both of them did. Cora and the two Mollies apparently employed some of the same girls and may even have operated in partnership from time to time.) The witnesses, however, proved unnecessary in the case against Cora Johnson; she failed to appear and was sentenced to forfeiture of the recognizance bond.

Near the same time that A.S. Johnson was putting up a bond for his wife, he also made his appearance in Jasper County Circuit Court as a defendant for the first time, in connection with a December 1877 charge of selling liquor on Sunday. Like many other activities in early-day Joplin, the goings-on at the Vaudeville Theatre were scarcely deterred by the occasion of the Sabbath.

A report in the December 21, 1877 issue of the *Daily Herald* suggests the flavor of entertainment that Joplin's early-day theatergoers might have witnessed at the Vaudeville:

The increased attractions at the Vaudeville brought out a full house last night. The singing by Miss Flora Franks, the "song bird of America," was fine, especially a comic song, which brought the house down and convulsed even the bald-heads in front. The clown act, by Billy Forrest and Mons. Searles, was new and added considerably to the attractions of the evening. The pantomime, "Marco the Dwarf," was presented in better shape than on previous occasions. Jennie Howard, as the innocent maiden, Mr. Frye the tormenter of "Marco" and "Daddy" Thompson, the father of sixteen children,

Sketch of an 1879 vaudeville and burlesque performer from the *National Police Gazette*.

besides the baby, Billy Forrest, as "Marco," all appeared unusually funny and entered into the play with spirit.

The Vaudeville Theatre drew well throughout most of its stay in Joplin. Full houses were not unusual, even though the theater was open nearly every night of the week. In late December 1877, *Hawkeye the Scout* played to a full house, despite "the bad weather and semi-liquid condition of the streets and crossings." When a new production called *Led Astray* opened at the

Vaudeville in early January of the following year, it faced competition from other entertainment venues like the Opera House. Located in the upstairs of a building near the corner of Second and Main Streets in West Joplin, the latter facility tended to cater to a more sophisticated audience and to offer more refined presentations like lectures and literary readings than the Vaudeville, but the average Joplinite apparently preferred slapstick to subtlety. "No matter what the number of counter attractions or what the inducements they may offer to the curiosity, pleasure or amusement seeker," remarked a *Daily Herald* reporter the day after *Led Astray* opened, "Vaudeville claims her full share. Last night was no exception, and a full house enjoyed the drama, laughed at the minstrel eccentricities or wondered at the trapeze performance, as each in succession was presented."

A.S. Johnson made periodic trips to large cities to secure new talent for his vaudeville show. In early February 1878, for instance, he went to Kansas City and brought back seriocomic vocalist Jennie Southern, among other performers. Later in the year, "the great Negro delineator" Billy Diamond, sometimes called "the black Diamond of America," played to full houses on Joplin's Broadway. "He can beat any man rattling the bones that ever visited Joplin," opined the *Daily Herald*, "and his songs and delineations are simply great."

Sometime during the middle part of 1878, A.S. Johnson moved his variety show from Broadway to another location in Joplin, and he may have suspended operations altogether for a while. By early November, however, he was reportedly moving the theater back "to its former location on Broadway."

While the vaudeville players were in Joplin for an extended run at the variety theater or at the end of such a run, Johnson would sometimes schedule additional performances at surrounding towns. For instance, on November 21, Johnson took his vaudeville troupe to the neighboring mining town of Galena, Kansas. He was soon back in Joplin, though, where his troupe, including his band, played in late December and where Johnson himself was up to his old tricks of selling liquor on Sunday. He paid a fifteen-dollar fine for the indiscretion.

In March 1879, A.S. Johnson made a trip to St. Louis and Cincinnati to engage new talent. He brought back song and dance man Ollie Audley, song and dance woman Josie Carroll, seriocomic vocalist Nellie Steele, and John and Hattie Smith, who were billed as "Negro comedians and song and dance artists." At a performance a few days after the new artists arrived, the Vaudeville drew its largest crowd in several months, and according to a *Daily Herald* reporter, the show was "never excelled in the West." The newspaperman also claimed at the same time that the Vaudeville band "gets more music out of a few instruments than any other band in the Southwest."

In addition to keeping a saloon adjacent to his theater, A.S. Johnson also started tending a beer garden in May 1879 at Castle Rock, a park or resort on Turkey Creek near where present-day St. Louis Street crosses the stream. The venture, however, put him at odds with local law enforcement, who apparently had decided about this time to clamp down on vice throughout the whole town. Johnson was cited for selling beer at the garden on three successive Sundays in late May and early June, and about half the sinners of Joplin were named on the same indictment with him for various offenses. Among those cited for liquor violations were Henry Sapp, S. Landauer, Gottlieb Schmierer, Herman Geldmacher, and Thomas Connor. Mollie Tate, Emma Ensling(er), and Lillie Wiggans were cited for keeping bawdyhouses, while Colonel Jennison and Bud Fagg were among those mentioned in connection with gambling. The outcome of Johnson's case is not known, but whatever penalty he might have paid did not deter him from continuing to run the beer garden during the summer of 1879.

On the night of November 17, 1879, the brass band that Johnson employed in conjunction with his vaudeville stirred up the town when it marched down Main Street in West Joplin and got into a noisy competition with another band that was playing at the Opera House at the time. A *Daily Herald* reporter described the scene in the next day's newspaper:

> *There was fun in Joplin last night...Any meteors wandering around in space within four hundred miles of the earth certainly would have been shaken down out of the sky by the stupendous noise that rent the atmosphere of this city last night about seven o'clock. Just think of two full brass bands coming together in the middle of the street, both playing different tunes as loud as they could roar. It was a sight and sound never to be forgotten...Golden's band stood in front of the Opera House, and Johnson's band came marching down Main Street playing some lively air. Just as the latter band got in front of Landauer's wholesale liquor house, Golden's band opened out on a rattling tune. Johnson's band looked upon this as a challenge, and stopping on the sidewalks in front of Sapp's saloon, fairly raised the awning from the posts. Then the fun began. The noise that rent the damp night air made the windows rattle for blocks around, and started all the dogs in East Joplin to howling. It was an amusing sight. The musicians bowed up their backs and blew until their eyes popped out and their cheeks looked like young balloons. A large*

crowd gathered on the sidewalks and added to the general clamor by cheering vociferously. After blowing and pounding for about twenty minutes Johnson's band walked slowly out into the street and stood side by side with the other band. The excitement by this time was intense. Men waved their hats and yelled themselves hoarse, while the younger generation went wild. Neither band would give in, and the racket increased until finally Marshal Hamilton interfered and Golden's band stopped playing, and the other band resumed their march down the street.

A few days after the lively competition, the *Daily Herald* reported that, in the future, the vaudeville band "will not parade on the streets of Joplin for reasons best known to Mr. Johnson." Presumably, after the rambunctious display on the night of the seventeenth, Marshal Hamilton or some other city official had ordered Johnson to keep his band off the streets.

In early 1879, a *Daily Herald* reporter, in commenting upon a performance at the Vaudeville Theatre, remarked that "the best of order was retained." The fact that the newspaperman considered good behavior at the theater noteworthy suggests that the Vaudeville was not a place where decorum was normally maintained. Sometimes, too, patrons of the Johnsons' establishment exhibited more than just bad manners.

In early to mid-October 1877, Frank Carney, a brother of Cora Johnson, arrived from Ohio to visit his sister and began helping out at the Vaudeville during his stay in Joplin. Between five and six o'clock on the morning of October 17, 1877, about a week after Carney's arrival, an intoxicated man named George O'Bannon stumbled into the saloon and knocked over a stove, scattering fire and ashes on the floor. Carney tried to get the man to clean up the mess and got into a violent argument with him. When O'Bannon called Carney a son of a bitch, Carney knocked him down and began beating him, but O'Bannon pulled a knife and stabbed his assailant. O'Bannon was quickly arrested and lodged in jail, and Carney, although seriously wounded, revived enough during the next few days that he was expected to make a full recovery.

Then, in the wee hours of the morning on December 18, 1879, a "shooting act" occurred at the Vaudeville that, according to the *Daily Herald*, was "not down on the programme." About 2:00 a.m., Cora Johnson entered the saloon, announced that it was time to close, and retrieved the key to the front door from Johnny Manning, the bartender. The only customers in the barroom, besides a few theater people who were staying with the Johnsons, were two young hellions named Billy Beck and Charles Marshall, the latter of whom had been arrested and lodged briefly in jail just the previous day for drunkenness and disorderly conduct. When Mrs. Johnson started toward the door to lock up, one of the young men told her not to be so fast because they wanted something more to drink. Apparently willing to stay open a while longer, Cora sat down at a table where a couple of the theater employees were playing cards.

Beck, a local boy, then inquired whether his credit was good for a couple of drinks, and Cora told him no. When he replied with "profane and indecent language," the bartender intervened and herded Beck out of the building while Cora went behind the bar to secure the day's receipts from the money till. While Manning was scuffling with Beck just outside the door, Marshall, who had followed the two outside, drew a revolver and fired at Manning, the ball ripping into a nearby sidewalk. The bartender ducked back into the saloon, and Beck rushed in behind him and tried to intercept Cora at the end of the bar. Meanwhile, Marshall appeared in the doorway, presented his pistol, and fired. The ball struck a mirror near Cora's head, shattering the glass into pieces, and Cora dashed into an adjoining room. The two hell-raisers then left, and A.S. Johnson appeared on the scene with a double-barrel shotgun and gave chase.

The two young men escaped to West Joplin, where Beck was arrested almost immediately and placed in the calaboose. Marshall was apprehended several hours later after he was spotted ducking into Geldmacher's saloon and exiting the rear door into an alley, where he was found hiding in an outhouse. In January 1880, Cora testified against Marshall at his preliminary hearing on a charge of assault with intent to kill.

When the 1880 census was taken in early June, A.S. and Cora Johnson were living on Broadway just a couple doors down from Emma Enslinger's bawdyhouse. The forty-two-year-old A.S. Johnson listed his profession as "theatrical manager," while the thirty-five-year-old Cora gave her occupation as "keeping house." Listed in the Johnson household were a large number of boarders whose occupations ranged from bartender to actor. (The *Daily Herald* had reported a few months earlier that A.S. Johnson employed fifty-three people in various capacities.)

One of Johnson's employees was gambler Jake Pecora, who, in partnership with a man named Al Searle, had recently started running a lunch counter at the Vaudeville saloon. On Sunday, June 27, however, the two partners got into a disagreement and ended up, according to the *Daily Herald*, indulging in "a first class row." During the mêlée, Pecora drew a pistol, but Searle kicked it out of his hand, causing it to go off, and the ball struck Searle in the foot. Pecora was arrested and charged with felonious assault. Among the witnesses for the state in the case were Thomas Carney, a second brother of Cora Johnson; and Allie Rogers, the same soiled dove who was later implicated in the larceny case against Emma Enslinger. Those testifying for the defense, on the other hand, included the notorious Pink Fagg, whose brother Bud was also implicated in the Enslinger case. Perhaps Pink proved persuasive because charges against Pecora were eventually dropped.

About the time the June 1880 census was taken, A.S. Johnson announced that he had leased an opera house at the booming mineral-water town of Eureka Springs, Arkansas, and he was going to run it as a legitimate theater and give up vaudeville altogether.

Apparently, his plans fell through or were delayed, however, because he hung around Joplin a good while longer. In mid-July 1880, he and his vaudeville troupe were "entertaining the boys of Short Creek" at Galena. "Johnson always gets up a good show," proclaimed the *Galena Miner*, "and his houses show that they are appreciated."

In December 1880, Johnson and his vaudeville were back in Joplin, where they continued to amuse theatergoers for a few more months. Then, in the spring of 1881, Johnson sold his theater and the adjoining saloon to Jake Pecora, who promptly changed the establishment's name to the Theatre Comique. The Johnsons, however, maintained their residence next to the theater building.

On June 6, while A.S. Johnson was on a trip to Eureka Springs not long after the theater had changed hands, Tom Carney went to Pecora's saloon and started to take some silverware that he claimed belonged to his sister and her husband. Pecora said he owned the silverware because it came with the property he had purchased, and the two men got into a violent argument. Whether prior bad blood between the two men as a result of Carney's testimony against Pecora the previous year contributed to the heated dispute is unknown.

At any rate, when the argument escalated, Pecora called on Frank Wollard, a "stout negro" in his employ, for help, and Wollard put Carney out. Infuriated, Carney went next door to his sister's house to get a pistol. Cora tried to keep him from taking it, but he wrenched it away from her and headed back to the saloon, where Wollard met him at the door. When Carney presented the weapon, Wollard swatted it away, but the pistol went off, wounding Wollard in the leg. With Wollard incapacitated, Carney pointed his weapon toward Pecora and opened fire. Pecora returned fire, and approximately eight shots were fired in all. In the crossfire a black man named Charles Thompson, a performer at the Theatre Comique, was hit and mortally wounded, and a coroner's jury later determined that Thompson had come to his death at the hands of Thomas Carney. Although Carney was also hit and seriously injured, it was thought at first that he would recover, and he was charged with murder. After lingering throughout the summer, however, he died in late August before the case could come to trial.

Although A.S. Johnson was no longer proprietor of the Vaudeville, his wife, Cora, continued to entertain Joplin in her own way for a while longer. In late 1881, she was cited in circuit court for having kept a bawdyhouse on July 1, 1881, and at "divers other times." Shortly after the July 1 date, however, Cora and her husband sold their remaining property on Broadway to beer king Charley Schifferdecker, presumably in preparation of moving away, and it's unclear exactly how much longer they remained in Joplin. In June 1882, Cora was again charged with the misdemeanor of running a house of ill fame, the last mention of either her or her husband in Jasper County records, but she and Augustus might have already taken their leave of Joplin prior to the indictment being brought.

A.S. and Cora Johnson were rather obscure figures in the overall history of Joplin. They have been scarcely mentioned in previous commentaries on the town's past, and they would probably be stunned to learn that someone has chronicled their story over 125 years after the fact. But in 1870s Joplin, the Johnsons' Vaudeville Variety Theatre was the place to be for rowdy miners looking for ribald entertainment.

JOE THORNTON

A DESPERADO OF THE WORST CHARACTER

I am too lazy to work and too "ornery" to live.
If you want to "send me over the road" I'm ready.
—Joe Thornton, facing a Joplin lynch mob in 1885,
as quoted in the Daily Herald

From its very founding in the early 1870s, Joplin was a rowdy town that witnessed more than its share of fisticuffs, knife fights, and gunplay. To describe or even try to list all the violent episodes in the town's history is beyond the scope of this work, but a few stand out as particularly notorious. One affair that occurred in 1885 during Joplin's early years still ranks among the town's most infamous more than 125 years later. The incident was authored by a desperate character named Joe Thornton, but the townspeople themselves wrote the final chapter.

Thornton came to southeast Kansas in the stampede that followed the discovery of lead on Short Creek in the spring of 1877. Arriving in the Galena area with his parents, the twenty-six-year-old Thornton took up mining alongside his father and brothers, and he was considered an ordinary young man whose "early life...would compare favorably with that of other young men." About the time his parents moved to Arkansas around 1880, though, Joe "took to drink and associating with lewd women," and he decided that selling liquor was an easier way of making a living than mining lead.

A bill prohibiting the sale of liquor in Kansas took effect in the spring of 1881, but not long afterward a few Galena businessmen decided to circumvent the new law by starting a "town" on the nearby border of Missouri, where liquor was legal (but, unlike in Kansas, gambling was not). Officially called Dubuque but more commonly known as Budgeville or Budgetown, the place consisted in the late spring of 1881 of two saloons and a couple of other businesses. Later, Thornton took possession of one of the saloons, a double building that straddled the state line with one half of it in Kansas and the other half in Missouri, and by the mid-1880s his was the only business left in Budgetown. Called the State Line House, the building was a saloon on the Missouri side, while the Kansas half served as a gambling house.

Thornton apparently neglected to acquire the proper permit in Missouri when he took over the saloon because a recurring complaint against him in Jasper County during the early to mid-1880s was selling liquor without a license. Rarely, though, were formal charges brought, or if they were, they were routinely dismissed upon payment of a fine.

However, Thornton soon earned a reputation as a "desperado of the worst character," and his "dive" on the state line was reputed to be the "resort of bad men and lewd women" where "disgraceful brawls and fights" were a frequent occurrence. One report suggested that Thornton had killed a man in Texas, but the claim was disputed. The Thornton family did live briefly in Texas before coming to Kansas, but Joe Thornton's murderous shenanigans in the Lone Star State may have been a figment of his own "would-be-desperado" imagination or an embellishment that was added by others to amplify his infamous reputation after he had become notorious in the Joplin area.

On September 29, 1884, Thornton came to Joplin and made a "threatening display of a pistol" toward a hack driver named George Simpson. Joplin city marshal Cass Hamilton was informed of the fact, and he found Thornton sitting on the edge of the platform at the Gulf Railroad depot with his revolver in his hand. When Hamilton walked up and told Thornton he was under arrest, the latter immediately shoved the pistol against the marshal's side and snapped it twice. Miraculously, though, the cartridges failed to fire, and Thornton was quickly subdued with "a well-directed blow" and lodged in jail. Brought before the Joplin police court the next day on a charge of carrying a concealed weapon, he was fined $200, plus costs, the maximum penalty the city court could assess. Unable to pay the fine, he was lodged in the city jail, and a state warrant was also served on him for his attempt on Marshal Hamilton's life. A report at the time said that the latter case would be adjudicated once the city case was disposed of, but instead the charge was apparently dropped, because Thornton was soon a free man once again.

A couple of months later, on Saturday, December 6, he rode into Galena armed with two revolvers and boisterously announced that he had just killed a man named Jim Ginn at his state line saloon for "monkeying with" his wife. Thornton made some threats about what he would do if anyone tried to arrest him for the deed and then summoned a doctor and rode back to Budgetown. When Dr. Walker of Galena reached the scene, he found that Ginn, a miner from nearby Lehigh, was alive and had not even been shot; rather, Thornton had knocked him down with a pistol, badly bruising his head and face.

In early 1885, Thornton again antagonized authorities when he was implicated as an accessory after the fact in a minor crime. When a man named Miner stole thirty-five dollars in Galena and made a getaway, law officers in Joplin were alerted to be on the lookout for the fugitive, and he was arrested there on February 23 and relieved of a "big hungry-looking pistol and a belt filled with cartridges," which he was sporting at the time. Further investigation revealed that Joe Thornton had supplied Miner with the weapon and ammunition after the robbery.

Spurred perhaps by Thornton's more recent misdeeds, Jasper County officials formally indicted him in March 1885 for selling liquor without a license the previous year. The complaint specified that he had, at an undesignated date in 1884, hawked a pint of whiskey, a pint of brandy, a pint of gin, a pint of wine, and a pint of lager beer.

It was not, however, until Saturday, July 18, 1885, when Thornton made a trip to Joplin that authorities tried to serve the warrant. He came into town aboard a buggy in the late afternoon accompanied by "the woman who claims to be his wife." Upon alighting from the buggy, he made a demonstration of taking a revolver from his pocket and placing it under the seat of the buggy, as if to give the impression that he was disarming himself.

As Thornton and his companion strolled up Main Street, stopping at various shops to make small purchases, they were spotted by Sergeant Daniel Sheehan of the Joplin city police. A citizen informed Sheehan that Thornton was unarmed, but the officer, having been instructed by Marshal Hamilton not to try to apprehend the desperado alone if he ever showed up in town, trailed the couple from a distance as they continued north on Main Street. When Thornton and the woman entered Schwartz's dry goods store at the corner of Second and Main, Sheehan saw Jasper County deputy sheriff Julius C. Miller across the street at the post office and went over to inform him of Thornton's whereabouts. The two lawmen were joined there by a third officer, George McMurtry of the Joplin police.

Miller, who was bearing the warrant for Thornton's arrest on the liquor charge, said he would go into the store and make the arrest if the other two men would back him up, and they agreed. McMurtry stood at the door while the other two lawmen entered the store. They spotted Thornton in the millinery department with his wife and approached him from behind. Miller tapped the desperado on the shoulder and asked if his name was Thornton.

When Thornton turned to face the two lawmen and answered "yes," Miller announced that he had a warrant for his arrest and grasped his right arm, while Sheehan took hold of his left. Thornton moved a step or two toward the door as though he were going to go with the lawmen willingly, then suddenly jerked his right arm free and whipped out a .45-caliber self-cocking revolver, which he had concealed in the front of his pants.

Before he could use the weapon, Miller wrapped both arms around him from behind and grabbed the pistol with both hands, while Sheehan began trying to pry the weapon from Thornton's grip. The desperate Thornton had the weapon pointed toward Sheehan's body when McMurtry came rushing up and, noticing the villain's finger on the trigger, struck the muzzle a downward blow to try to deflect the path of the bullet just as the pistol fired. He was too late, though, and the bullet tore through Sheehan's body.

Despite being seriously wounded, Officer Sheehan momentarily held his grip on the weapon. McMurtry, who was not armed, struck Thornton a powerful blow on the side of the head with his fist, sending all three of the other men staggering through an opening in one of the store's counters, and they collapsed behind the counter in a heap with Sheehan on the bottom, Thornton in the middle, and Miller on top.

Thornton, the "human tiger," began savagely biting Miller's hands to try to get him to relax his grip on the revolver, but the deputy held on, knowing that to let go would mean sure death. Meanwhile, a couple of bystanders moved one of the counters out of the way so that Officer McMurtry could reach the other three men, and he retrieved Sheehan's club from beneath "the human heap." In reaching for it, he received a bite from Thornton's teeth, but he promptly "commenced belaboring the criminal's head" with the club. Thornton cried out with each blow, and blood started spurting from his head, but he continued biting and clawing to try to loosen Miller's grip. McMurtry's space to work was so cramped that he accidently hit Miller a blow on the head that almost caused him to release his grip.

When the deputy called on some of the bystanders to help, one of them moved another counter out of the way, and a second one finally managed to get the pistol out of Thornton's loosened grip. Seeing that further resistance was futile, Thornton quit struggling and was dragged out and taken to the city jail, located on Second Street just a couple of doors from the dry goods store.

After Thornton was taken off, Officer Sheehan stood up and leaned against a counter, turning deathly pale. Only then did onlookers realize that he had

Monument to Daniel Sheehan placed at Fairview Cemetery by the people of Joplin shortly after his death.

been seriously wounded, and he was quickly taken to Dr. Robert Kelso's nearby office. The doctor treated the wound but pronounced it mortal, and the injured man was later carried to his home.

Upon learning that Sergeant Sheehan's wound would almost certainly prove fatal, a crowd that had gathered around the jail continued to linger late into the evening brooding over the news. Gradually, though, the crowd dispersed, until what remained in the wee hours of Sunday morning, July 19, was a small, ugly mob. Near 2:00 a.m., about fifteen to twenty masked men approached the jail from an alley carrying a piece of heavy timber and started battering the front door of the jail. The noise attracted a few onlookers, but they were warned away with a flourish of revolvers.

The mob quickly gained entrance to the jailhouse and overpowered the guards. They knocked the lock off Thornton's cell with a pick. The desperado reportedly greeted them with a show of bravado, baring his chest, taunting the vigilantes with curses, and daring them to shoot him, but they had other plans. They dragged him from the cell, looped a rope over his head, and led him half a block to the corner of Second and Joplin Streets, where stood a house surrounded by maple trees. They tossed the end of the rope over a limb of one of the maples and asked their prisoner if he had any last words to say. "Gentlemen," Thornton replied, "I don't think I have been fairly treated, but I die game."

According to a Joplin newspaper, "The order was then given to pull, a dozen strong arms instantly obeyed the order, and the body of Joe Thornton was suspended between heaven and earth."

The executioners slipped away into the night, and a crowd once again gathered, gaping in awe as Thornton's body dangled beneath the maple limbs. The county sheriff showed up a few minutes later and cut the corpse down. Officer Sheehan died about eight hours later, about 10:00 a.m. on Sunday morning. The same day, July 19, friends and relatives of Thornton came over from Galena to take charge of his body, and a coroner's jury met and arrived at a verdict that the "deceased came to an untimely end by hanging at the hands of parties whom the jury did not have the honor to know."

THE INFAMOUS HOUSE OF LORDS

The House of Lords had a big name for glittering swank and I had to see it.
—*Thomas Hart Benton, writing in* An Artist in America *of his experience in Joplin during the summer of 1906*

In the early 1920s, after Prohibition had forced the House of Lords Saloon and the gambling room above it to close, all that remained of the renowned establishment was the House of Lords Café. When the café also finally closed its doors in early 1922, the *Joplin Globe* commented that its demise brought to an end "one of the most famous resorts in the United States, or, perhaps, the world." Lamenting that the once splendid House of Lords had been reduced, at its closing, to a mere café, the *Globe* article vividly recalled the glory days of the establishment:

> When into the memory comes a scene with a gambling house, containing every device that worshipers at the shrine of the Goddess of Chance could desire; with a saloon where the choicest of whiskies and the rarest of wines, as well as virtually all other alcoholic beverages were dispensed; with booths where political bosses conferred with their minions and hatched schemes for gaining or retaining power; with a restaurant where nightly orgies culminated on New Year's Eve in a Bacchanalian revel that knew no bounds; with rooms above where broken flowers from the primrose path sent forth their siren call—when a composite picture

Interior of the House of Lords, circa 1910. *Courtesy Joplin Historical and Mineral Museums, Inc.*

of such a place is in one's mind, then that is the House of Lords as it was at the zenith of its existence.

The House of Lords was opened as a saloon at 319 Main Street in Joplin about 1891 by William B. Patton, who gave the place its aristocratic name a few months later. Patton reportedly held a contest of sorts to name the place, inviting early customers to place their suggestions in a fish bowl so that he could draw them out until he discovered one he liked. When he drew out "House of Lords," which had been placed in the bowl by an Englishman who was staying at the nearby Keystone Hotel at the time, Patton liked the name so well that he had a royal crest and the words "House of Lords" inscribed in the floor of the saloon entryway.

About a year after starting his saloon, Patton opened a café and billiard hall in the adjoining room at 321 Main Street, and a door connected the two businesses. Both the saloon and the café were located toward the rear of the building, while a cigar stand and other businesses occupied a shallow block of rooms along the front of the building. To reach the café from the front entrance, customers followed a corridor that ran along the south part of the building, while a similar passageway along the north led to the saloon. At the front entrance, a stairway led to a gambling room on the second floor, and "those who wanted to keep climbing," according to Jones's *Tales About Joplin*, could reach a third floor populated by scarlet ladies. A stairway to the upper rooms was also conveniently located at the saloon.

The café developed a reputation not only for its fine food but also as a place where power brokers met and hashed out mining deals and other business transactions over a sumptuous meal and a glass of wine. Meanwhile, the gambling house above the saloon, which was under separate management from the bar and café, became known for its high-stakes games of chance and the third-floor brothel for its supposedly classy prostitutes.

Patton sold the saloon and café after a few years, and a succession of owners held the place for brief periods of time until Edward C. Peregoy and Jesse McCullough took over shortly after the turn of the twentieth century and ran the businesses for the remainder of their existence. The first manager of the second-floor gambling room, Billy Hunter, also left after a brief time, and a string of other men took charge of that operation as well.

The real mover and shaker behind the House of Lords, though, was Gilbert "Gid" Barbee, owner of the building that housed it. Barbee, like a number of Joplin's other leading citizens at the turn of the century, had come to the town during its very early days and gotten wealthy through mining interests. A staunch Democrat, he was Joplin's first political boss and also part owner of the *Joplin Globe*. He had his living quarters in the *Globe* building behind the House of Lords, and he had a walkway built across the alley from his apartment as a convenient access to the second floor of the House of Lords building, where the gambling room and, later, a dining room were located. The violence that sometimes took place in the House of Lords saloon and the questionable enterprises in other parts of the building made Barbee an occasional object of satire from rival newspapers because of his close association with the place.

Anecdotal stories suggesting the legendary goings-on at the House of Lords abound. According to Shaner's *Story of Joplin*, for instance, sometimes as much as $50,000 might change hands during a weekend poker game at the gambling room above the saloon. During the 1890s, the gambling room served as the Joplin headquarters of the infamous Buckfoot gang of swindlers, whose scams mainly involved betting on rigged footraces, and the saloon and the gambling room also witnessed a number of serious fights, including three killings. Although little is known about the activities on the third floor, the 1922 *Globe* article confirmed that, unlike the male domains of the saloon and the gambling room, the café was frequented by both "society women and demimondaine." The two classes of women, however, "remained well within their respective spheres." Shaner also recalled that "denizens of the red light district" patronized the House of Lords Café, and he described exactly what staying within one's own sphere entailed. The women of ill fame, he explained, were always seated at a table situated in a corner away from the other customers, and they were "conspicuous because of their ostrich plumed hats, French heels, and rouged cheeks."

In 1906, seventeen-year-old aspiring artist Thomas Hart Benton left his Neosho home and got a job for the summer working on a surveying crew at Joplin. The lively mining town impressed the seventeen-year-old lad: "The saloon doors—and there were plenty of them—swung constantly...Everything was there—drugstores, slot machines, real-estate slickers, soliciting preachers, and off the main street, a row of houses devoted to insinuatingly decorated girls." On Saturday nights, young Benton went downtown and drank beer in the saloons like a grown man, but he avoided the House of Lords during his first few visits because he knew it was a gathering place not only for miners and roughnecks but also for "substantial businessmen," and he didn't want to take a chance of meeting someone who might recognize him and treat him as a boy or, worse yet, patronize him only because he was a member of the well-to-do Benton family. One Saturday, though, he finally decided he had to see the House of Lords, and he sauntered into the saloon and ordered a beer. As he sat at the bar, his attention was soon absorbed by a painting of a masked naked lady that hung on the wall. Noticing the newcomer's rapt attention to the nude portrait, a group of men lining the bar next to Benton began laughing and making fun of him. Embarrassed, Benton said he wasn't particularly interested in the naked girl but was studying the portrait from an artistic standpoint.

"So, you're an artist, Shorty?" gibed one of the men.

"Yes, by God! I am," Benton retorted.

One of the men told him there was a new newspaper starting up in Joplin, and he challenged Benton to go apply for a job as a sketch artist. The young man took the dare and, somewhat to his own surprise, landed the job. Benton, of course, went on to become one of the most famous American artists of the twentieth century, and years later when he wrote his autobiography, he looked back at his experience at the infamous House of Lords saloon as the starting point of his career.

Although anecdotes like Benton's are plentiful, hard facts supporting the mythology of orgies and revels at the House of Lords are scant. Court records show that Peregoy, the House of Lords' saloonkeeper, was charged in 1903 with keeping a gaming house, and his partner, McCullough, was named as a security on the bond. The specification was that Peregoy had allowed men to

The 300 block of Main Street in Joplin, 1907, showing the House of Lords sign on the left. *Courtesy of Galen Augustus.*

gamble on a game of cards in his establishment. Also, Peregoy and McCullough were charged multiple times over the next few years for selling liquor on Sunday. However, these several citations against Peregoy and McCullough appear to be the only violations mentioned in Jasper County Court records that are associated with the House of Lords saloon, and contemporaneous evidence pertaining to the upper rooms of the building is even scarcer than documentation relating to the saloon.

For instance, proof that the third floor of the House of Lords building was a bawdyhouse appears to be negligible to nonexistent. Houses of ill repute certainly operated throughout downtown Joplin during the entire period that the House of Lords saloon was open, but the ones mentioned in Jasper County Circuit Court records were associated with addresses like 206 Pennsylvania, where madam Flora Summers ruled the house, and 201 Main, where Jane DeChancey reigned, not with 319 Main Street. So, we are left only with after-the-fact reminiscences like the 1922 *Globe* article to support the House of Lords' infamous reputation as a shrine to the gods of pleasure.

Perhaps the dearth of contemporaneous evidence is due in part to the fact that the House of Lords was, as the *Globe* reporter pointed out, a place where men who wielded political power, like Gid Barbee, hung out. It's not unlikely, therefore, that city authorities might have turned a blind eye to the goings-on at the place. It's also probable, however, that the notorious reputation of the place has been exaggerated. If the city police turned a blind eye to the shenanigans on the upper floors of the House of Lords, one might reasonably ask, why did they not also overlook Peregoy and McCullough's minor indiscretions of selling liquor on Sunday? It's interesting to note that Benton, in his recollection about the House of Lords, made no mention of gambling rooms or third-floor girls. Even the 1922 *Globe* article, Shaner's *Story of Joplin*, and Jones's *Tales About Joplin* seem to intimate that the third floor of the House of Lords building was not a bawdyhouse in the same sense as Emma Enslinger's place on Broadway back in the 1870s and 1880s. More likely, it was a place of assignation where women whom today we might consider "escorts" or call girls rendezvoused with their clients. As Jones suggested, it was a place to which common streetwalkers might aspire but where only the "really good bad girls" were accepted. It almost certainly was not a bordello overseen by a madam who lived full time on the premises with a stable of prostitutes.

Peregoy and McCullough ran both the House of Lords saloon and the café/billiard parlor until Prohibition forced them to close the saloon. At that time, they moved the café, name and all, to 407 Main Street, where it stayed until its 1922 closing as recounted in the *Globe* article.

The legend of the House of Lords has no doubt grown over the years, but it hardly matters whether all the fabled goings-on in the various parts of the establishment can be confirmed today. The House of Lords, even during its existence, was always as much about reputation as reality.

ONE OF THOSE HOT SPOTS YOU GET INTO AND CAN'T GET OUT OF

BONNIE AND CLYDE'S JOPLIN SHOOTOUT

Clyde Barrow did not choose Joplin at random. It was known then as "a
wide-open town," used by members of the underworld like Pretty Boy Floyd,
the Barker brothers, and Alvin Karpis as a safe haven.
—John Neal Phillips in Blanche Caldwell Barrow's
My Life with Bonnie and Clyde

The day after Tom DeGraff and four other lawmen shot it out in Joplin with the notorious Bonnie and Clyde gang, DeGraff described the encounter as a "hot spot" or "just one of those places you get into and can't get out of." Fortunately for DeGraff, he *was* able to get out of the situation alive, but for two of his comrades, Wes Harryman and Harry McGinnis, the deadly encounter proved, indeed, to be a place they couldn't get out of. If the five lawmen had known the desperate character of the people they were dealing with, they might not have gotten into the "hot spot," and Harryman and McGinnis, too, might have lived to tell the story.

Because Joplin's reputation as a wide-open town persisted into the 1920s and 1930s, notorious gangsters from the era sometimes hid out in the region. For instance, the Barker boys, who lived at Webb City during their youth, repeatedly returned to the Joplin-Webb City area to lie low long after they had moved to Tulsa and become infamous as the Ma Barker gang. Joplin's history as a place where the law didn't ask too many questions and its location near two state lines made it an ideal hideout. Even if things happened to get hot, Oklahoma and Kansas were only five miles away.

Although they were from Texas, Bonnie and Clyde also made several forays into the Ozarks and became familiar with the Joplin area. In late November 1932, shortly after Clyde had formed his own gang, he, Bonnie, and two partners arrived in southwest Missouri and holed up in a Carthage motel. On November 29, Bonnie scouted out the Farmers and Miners Bank of Oronogo, about fifteen miles north of Joplin, and the next day Clyde and the two sidekicks robbed the bank and shot the place up. Eight weeks later, on January 26, 1933, Bonnie and Clyde, along with partner W.D. Jones, kidnapped Springfield motorcycle cop Thomas Persell and took him on a pell-mell journey across southwest Missouri, including a drive through the Roanoke neighborhood of north Joplin, before finally letting him out near Stone's Corner north of town.

Barely over two months later, on or about April 1, 1933, Bonnie, Clyde, and W.D. Jones were back in Joplin for an extended stay. The three were joined by Clyde's brother, Buck Barrow, and Buck's wife, Blanche. Just released from prison and newly pardoned by the Texas governor, Buck wanted to relax and catch up on old times with his brother. Using the name Callahan, he rented an apartment from Paul Freeman in the Freeman Grove addition of south

The house on Oak Ridge Drive in Joplin where the Bonnie and Clyde shootout occurred, as it appears today.

Joplin at 3347½ Oak Ridge Drive. Despite the address, the apartment was located over a two-car garage that faced Thirty-fourth Street. For the gang's purposes, it was ideally situated on the outskirts of town just a couple blocks from Main Street.

The gang used one of the spaces in the garage to park its stolen Ford V-8 sedan. The other space was reserved for Harold Hill, a tenant in a nearby house; so Buck rented a small garage nearby from another neighbor, Sam Langford, to park the Marmon he had bought upon his release from prison. This was the car the desperadoes mainly used during their stay in Joplin.

The gang members mostly kept to themselves and didn't arouse much suspicion at first. Neighbors noted, however, that they always kept their blinds drawn and that lights sometimes shone from the apartment very late at night. More curiously, the mysterious strangers always backed their car into the garage so that it would be headed out as though ready for a quick getaway.

The Barrow family later claimed that Buck had planned to go straight after he got out of prison and that part of the reason he wanted to meet with Clyde was to try to convince his brother to turn himself in and give up his life of crime. Although this report is dubious, apparently the gang did manage to avoid criminal activity for the first week or so after they arrived in Joplin. Buck drove his Marmon to nearby Kansas and got it licensed at Girard because he thought a Kansas license plate would arouse less suspicion than a Texas tag. Mostly, though, the men idled away the days playing cards, while the women cooked and served the meals. Bonnie used part of her spare time composing poems, and Blanche played solitaire or worked puzzles. When the group started running short on funds, however, they soon resorted to their old ways. Clyde and W.D. pulled off a couple of burglaries, including one at the Neosho Milling Company. The pair also stole another vehicle, a Ford Roadster, and Buck talked Hill into letting the gang park it in the second space below the apartment.

The increased comings and goings of the gang and the group's somewhat eccentric behavior gradually pricked the curiosity of neighbors, and one of them reported his suspicions to the Joplin branch of the Missouri Highway Patrol. The informer said the strangers at the Oak Ridge Drive apartment had switched license plates from one vehicle to another and had driven one of the cars without a license plate. Also, one of the vehicles matched the publicized description of an automobile that had been linked to the Neosho burglary. State troopers investigated and further learned that the Marmon had been licensed at Girard by a man named Barrow, even though the apartment had been rented under the name of Callahan.

Suspecting that the gang holed up there were either bootleggers or burglars, lawmen decided on April 13 to raid the place. Because the apartment was located in Newton County, state troopers G.B. Kahler and W.E. Grammer enlisted the help of Newton County constable J.W. "Wes" Harryman in obtaining a liquor search warrant, and they drove to Neosho to get the warrant. Back in Joplin, they were joined by Joplin police detectives Harry McGinnis and Tom DeGraff, and the five lawmen drove toward the Freeman Grove apartment about four o'clock in the afternoon. The two troopers were in one car with Kahler driving, while the other three men occupied a second car with DeGraff driving, Harryman riding shotgun, and McGinnis in the backseat. The two police cars turned off Main at Thirty-fourth Street and approached the apartment from the east with the troopers' car leading the way.

Clyde and W.D. had just returned from gallivanting as the police cars pulled up, and the lawmen spotted the pair still standing just inside the garage with the door partly open. Kahler pulled to a halt on Thirty-fourth just west of the building, while the officers in the trailing car took more direct action. Announcing that he would "head right in," DeGraff turned into the driveway as the man standing at the door attempted to close it. Harryman sprang out of the passenger's seat while the car was still rolling to a halt and lunged toward the door to try keep the suspect from closing it. From inside the garage, Clyde opened fire with a sawed-off shotgun, and W.D. began shooting with either a shotgun or an automatic rifle. Harryman collapsed at the garage doorway and died almost instantly.

As soon as DeGraff came to a halt, McGinnis jumped out of the backseat with a revolver in hand, and DeGraff exited the driver's side door. McGinnis managed to get off a couple of shots, one of which wounded Jones, but the officer was hit with a load of buckshot and stumbled back. Crouching beside the police car, DeGraff fired several shots and made his way to the rear of the vehicle, just as the mortally wounded McGinnis staggered and collapsed nearby.

The shooting had already started by the time Grammer jumped from the troopers' car and ran toward the back of the garage. Kahler quickly followed, taking up a vantage at the corner of a nearby house, where he commenced firing at one of the desperadoes he could see inside the garage. Meanwhile, DeGraff made his way around the east side of the garage, and when he saw Grammer at the rear of the building, he shouted for the trooper to go call for backup. Grammer hurried to the nearby Hill home to phone for reinforcements.

The situation inside the apartment was just as chaotic as it was outside. As soon as the shooting started, Buck, who had opened the garage door for Clyde and W.D. upon their return, rushed upstairs shouting to Blanche and Bonnie that the cops were here and the gang had to make a run for it. Buck then ran back downstairs and took W.D.'s weapon to reinforce Clyde, while Jones stumbled up the stairs clutching his wounded side and yelling for the women to hurry up and get in the car. Once downstairs, Bonnie jumped into the passenger's seat of the Ford sedan, while Blanche and the wounded Jones helped Clyde open the garage door.

Kahler, now the only officer at the front of the garage who was not either dead or dying, continued to menace the gangsters with pistol fire, and they directed their weapons toward him. A ricocheting bullet lodged just beneath Clyde's skin, and Buck was slightly grazed as lead flew all around. Clyde stepped from the garage firing his sawed-off shotgun, and Kahler began retreating and fell over a wire.

Photo of Clyde Barrow developed from film found in the Oak Ridge Drive apartment after the shootout. *Courtesy of Jasper County Records Center.*

Clyde, apparently thinking the officer was wounded, turned around and started back inside, and Kahler fired his last shot at the desperado.

Clyde, Blanche, and W.D. tried to push DeGraff's car out of the way, but they could not get the parking brake released. Clyde decided to push the police car out of the way with the gang's getaway car and ordered everyone into the Ford sedan. W.D. piled into the backseat as Buck pulled Harryman's body clear of the path between the two vehicles. Clyde, using the bumper of the Ford, knocked the police car loose, and it went careening down the sloped driveway. Blanche's little dog, Snow Ball, darted into the street at about the same time the police car coasted down the driveway, and already hysterical at the sight of the dead officers and the situation she found herself in, Blanche started after the dog. Buck called her back, though, and she and her husband piled into the backseat of the gangster car alongside W.D. The powerful V-8 Ford then roared away as Officers Kahler and DeGraff frantically reloaded their spent weapons and Grammer raced from the Hill home to belatedly join the fray. At the intersection of Thirty-fourth and Main, Clyde nodded to a garage man as he turned the corner and headed south out of town at a "mighty fast" rate of speed. The bandit car was traveling so fast by the time it reached Redings Mill, according to a service station attendant in the vicinity, that the driver almost lost control as he rounded the curve approaching the bridge over Shoal Creek. A few minutes later the gangsters zoomed through Seneca on their way to Texas.

Ambulances and additional police cars arrived on the scene at the Oak Ridge Drive apartment minutes after the shootout, but Harryman was already dead and the Barrow gang was long gone. McGinnis was rushed to a local hospital but died a few hours later.

Found inside the apartment were a cache of weapons and numerous other items the gang had abandoned in their haste to escape. The outlaw arsenal included an automatic rifle, four other high-powered rifles, a sawed-off shotgun, and a revolver. Among the other items left in the apartment was a badge of the Police and Sheriffs' Association of North America that officers believed the gang had used as a decoy in recent holdups, the marriage license of Buck Barrow and Blanche Caldwell, Buck's pardon from the Texas governor, some jewelry believed to have been taken in the Neosho Milling Company heist, a guitar, some letters and clothing, a bank bag of the McDaniel National Bank of Springfield, some "morbid and gangster poetry" including a verse called "Suicide Sal" that Bonnie had been working on, and a roll of undeveloped film that would soon make Bonnie and Clyde the most famous outlaws in America.

Developed by the *Joplin Globe*, the pictures included one of Bonnie playfully pointing a gun at Clyde and another of Bonnie striking a provocative pose with one leg hiked on the bumper of a car, a pistol in one hand and a cigar clenched between her teeth. Within days the photos were splashed on the front pages of newspapers across the country, and the Barrow gang members became not only some of the most wanted criminals in the United States but also almost instant folk heroes.

The death of Bonnie and Clyde by police ambush on a rural Louisiana road thirteen months after the Joplin shootout, of course, added to their tale of adventure, but it was the photos found in the Joplin apartment that started the legend to begin with. Without the Oak Ridge Drive pictures, members of the Barrow gang would likely have continued their criminal careers as the little-known hoodlums they were before April 13, 1933. It is almost certainly safe to say that without the Joplin film and the mischievous posing for the camera revealed therein, Bonnie and Clyde would not have become romantic figures of such stature to inspire popular Hollywood movies like the 1969 release starring Warren Beatty and Faye Dunaway.

Epilogue

JOPLIN'S REPUTATION
THROUGH THE YEARS

Joplin is "as bad as Babylon with its hanging gardens."
—*Dolph Shaner in* The Story of Joplin, *recalling the words of an unnamed temperance crusader circa 1910*

Even before it was formally incorporated in the early 1870s, Joplin had developed a reputation as a wide-open town, and by the mid- to late 1870s, that reputation was firmly established. In 1878, for instance, the *Springfield Times*, in discussing the "many questionable resorts" that abounded in Joplin, referred to its neighbor to the west as a "wicked city." Two years later, in 1880, the editor of the *Carthage Daily Patriot* expressed a similar view when he opined, "We fear that Joplin is a naughty place; so many naughty people live there!"

Citizens of Joplin recognized early on the disreputable name their town had gained in just a few short years. The editor of the *Daily Herald*, for instance, acknowledged in January 1880 that "Joplin has the name of a wicked city." Joplinites alternately resented and embraced the town's scandalous reputation. The *Herald* editor, for example, while arguing that the town's bad name was largely unwarranted, often took delight throughout the late 1870s and early 1880s in poking fun at other towns and especially at the editors of other towns' newspapers for their self-righteous attitudes. In 1890, the *Sunday Herald* editor had a good laugh at the expense of the holier-than-thou Kansas prohibitionists who came to Joplin and couldn't resist the temptations of the sinful city.

Joplin's reputation for depravity persisted throughout the next several decades and reached beyond the immediate region of southwest Missouri. In 1897, for instance, Ozarks author Nell M. Moore came to Missouri from Illinois as a young girl, and years later she recalled "the fear and trepidation with which my mothers and sisters first set foot on the 'ill reputed soil of Joplin.'"

In 1922, not long after Prohibition had taken effect, a satirical piece about Joplin and its reputation that appeared in the *Carthage Press* shed light not only on how others viewed Joplin but also on the mixed feelings of pride and defensiveness that Joplinites had about their own town:

> *If you have resided in this district more than two or three years you recall that Joplin, until quite recently, prided itself upon being a "wide-open" town. Apparently it catered to the saloon element, the gamblers, the prize fighters and the entire coterie of "easy come, easy go" citizenship incident to that sort of a town.*
>
> *Time was, not so long ago, when Joplin citizens referred laughingly to Carthage as the "holy city," because this town never had any ambition to be known as a frontier of civilization. Joplin intimated that one could not reside in Carthage long without sprouting wings and getting a halo. For many years three-fourths of the criminal cases in this county originated in Joplin...*
>
> *Joplin has apparently seen the error of her way. With the passing of the saloons, Joplin seems to have taken a new slant at the whole proposition. She has not yet taken the veil, but she certainly has begun to take notice of some conditions which would not have attracted a passing thought in "those good old days." She now is conducting a crusade against the "flappers!" Yes—at Joplin! The police are watching everything within a three-mile zone of Joplin and breaking up the "petting parties" in the shady lanes inside the city limits. Let it be known that Joplin doesn't intend to have any corruption of Joplin morals, if Joplin police can prevent it...*
>
> *It wouldn't seem so funny if it were almost any other town in the world, but Joplin! Shades of the House of Lords, Shades of the days of Buckfoot! Shades of the old free-and-easy "wide-open" town!*

Despite the Carthage newspaperman's parody on his neighboring town's newfound sense of morality, Joplin wasn't quite ready to discard its mantle as an anything-goes sort of place. It was partly its continued reputation as a wide-open town, of course, that drew gangsters like Bonnie and Clyde to Joplin during the Depression era of the 1930s.

Even during World War II, Joplin's raucous reputation was still alive and well, and it stretched far beyond the Ozarks, as the following anecdote from a current Joplin-area resident will illustrate. During the war, Maxine Hansford Gammon was a young army nurse stationed at Fitzsimmons General Hospital in Denver, Colorado, when word came that General Dwight D. Eisenhower would be giving an address via shortwave radio concerning the latest war news, and most of the army personnel stationed at the hospital gathered in an auditorium to listen to the talk. At one point during the speech, General Eisenhower announced that the ban on American GIs socializing with German frauleins had been lifted. "Now," proclaimed the general, "Berlin will be like Joplin, Missouri, on a Saturday night."

Maxine says that she remembers the incident so well because she had never heard of Joplin, Missouri, at the time. Little did she know that she would one day end up living in the wicked city.

BIBLIOGRAPHY

Barrow, Blanche Caldwell. *My Life with Bonnie and Clyde*. Edited by John Neal Phillips. Norman: University of Oklahoma Press, 2004.

Benton, Thomas Hart. *An Artist in America*. Columbia: University of Missouri Press, 1968.

Carthage Evening Press

Carthage People's Press

Carthage Weekly Banner

Galena [Kansas] *Miner*

Gammon, Maxine. Interview with author, June 23, 2010.

Greene County Circuit Court Records

Historic Joplin, www.historicjoplin.org.

Hounschell, Jim. *Lawmen and Outlaws: 116 Years in Joplin's History*. Marceline, MO: Walsworth Publishing Co., Inc., 1989.

Jasper County Circuit Court Records

Jasper County Probate Court Records

Jones, Evelyn Milligan. *Tales About Joplin Short and Tall*. Joplin, MO: Harragan House, 1962.

Joplin Court of Common Pleas Records

Joplin Daily Herald

Joplin Globe

Joplin Sunday Herald

Livingston, Joel. *A History of Jasper County and Its People*. 2 vols. Chicago: The Lewis Publishing Co., 1912.

McCullough, Florence Woodlock, comp. *Living Authors of the Ozarks and Their Literature.* Joplin, MO: Florence Woodlock McCullough, 1941.

Neosho Miner and Mechanic

Neosho Times

North, F.A. *History of Jasper County, Missouri.* Des Moines, IA: Mills and Co., 1883.

Phillips, John Neal. *Running with Bonnie and Clyde: The Ten Fast Years of Ralph Fults.* Norman: University of Oklahoma Press, 1996.

Shaner, Dolph. *The Story of Joplin.* New York: Stratford House, Inc., 1948.

Short Creek [Galena, Kansas] *Republican*

Springfield Times

State Line Herald, 1880–81

United States Census Records

ABOUT THE AUTHOR

L arry Wood is a retired public school teacher and freelance writer specializing in the history of the Ozarks region. His magazine articles have appeared in publications like *America's Civil War, Blue and Gray, Gateway Heritage, History Magazine, Kansas Heritage, Missouri Historical Review, Missouri Life, Ozarks Mountaineer, Ozarks Reader, Show Me the Ozarks, True West,* and *Wild West.* His previous books include *The Civil War on the Lower Kansas-Missouri Border, The Civil War Story of Bloody Bill Anderson, Other Noted Guerrillas of the Civil War in Missouri, Ozarks Gunfights and Other Notorious Incidents, The Two Civil War Battles of Newtonia,* and two historical novels entitled *Call Me Charlie: A Novel of a Quantrill Raider* and *Showdown at Baxter Springs.* Wood and his wife, Gigi, live in Joplin, Missouri.

Visit us at
www.historypress.net